SCHOOLING
FOR THE
LEARNING
DISABLED

SCHOOLING
FOR THE
LEARNING DISABLED

‖‖

A Selective Guide
to LD Programs in
Elementary and Secondary Schools
Throughout the United States

Compiled and Edited by
Raegene B. Pernecke and Sara M. Schreiner

with a foreword by Betty B. Osman

SMS Publishing Corporation

Ref
LC
4705
.P47
1983

Library of Congress Catalog Card No. 83-050934
FIRST TRADE EDITION
ISBN 0-914985-00-0

This book was set in Chicago by Law Bulletin Publishing Company. It was printed and bound by Pioneer Press Inc. of Wilmette, IL.

Foreword

Parents are naturally concerned about their children's learning and their education. Most young people in this country today are educated in a relatively smooth progression through the grades in their neighborhood public schools. In the course of this process, few major parental decisions or interventions are required.

When a child has a learning disability, though, parental responsibility and involvement in their children's education are greatly increased. Not only is their participation required each year in formulating the IEP (Individual Education Program), but they may also have to judge whether or not the school is meeting their child's needs. When a child is relatively happy in school and is progressing, parents, too, are usually content with the status quo. But when a child is miserable and/or does not seem to be benefitting from the education offered, parents may seek an alternative school setting. Selecting a school that is "right" for a youngster with learning disabilities presents a real challenge. Specialized private schools are, by and large, not well known, may be difficult to visit, and even harder for parents to assess.

This resource guide provides parents and other adults with useful information about alternative educational programs. This is a *different* kind of book about schools. It does not merely list schools with descriptions written by enthusiastic founders or administrators of the programs. Rather, it presents the observations of independent investigators who are themselves parents as well as professionals. Their accounts of the schools selected are informal, colorful, and insightful.

In using this guide, the reader will gain valuable information and a *feeling* about the schools reviewed, not readily gleaned from standard guides. This book is an important resource for parents in the process of choosing a school for the young person with learning disabilities.

Betty B. Osman, Ph.D.
Scarsdale, New York
October, 1983

5

Acknowledgments

We, the authors of this book, give credit to some very special people who helped bring our publication into being.

- To our husbands—for their love, patience, advice, humor and good will.
- To our children — for their smiling forebearance.
- To a father — for his guidance, faith and legacy.
- To a niece and nephew — for their inspiration.
- To a brother — for his kindness and judgment.
- To the investigative and journalistic team of Paula Dean, Clarence Hach, Betty Herrmann, Dorothy Lawson, Beth Mynhier and William Schreiner — for their jobs well done.
- To Dr. Jeanette Fleischner (Columbia Teachers College), Ms. Adele Handler (educational specialist), Dr. Robert Harth (National College of Education), Dr. William McLure (University of Illinois), and Dr. Mario Pascale (educational consultant) — for professional insights and assistance.
- To Betty Osman — for agreeing to review our manuscript.
- To Nancy Bauman, Pat Court, Gladys Cowman, Julie Grandmaison, Ruth MacCartney, Celestine Solheim — for their help beyond the call of duty.
- To Karen Stipp and Nancy Olderr — for fine, finishing manuscript touches.
- To Jack Ruggles and Dennis Beard — for their personal attention to our typesetting and printing needs.
- To Len Sider — for his photographic expertise.
- To Candice Cowman and Edie Ramsdell — for their artistic contributions.
- To Glenbrook South High School of Glenview, Illinois, and the Minnetonka (Minnesota) Public Schools — for their cooperation and the model they provided.
- To friends and relatives — for being there when we needed them.

To these people, we say *thank you.*

CONTENTS

▉▉

A SELECTIVE GUIDE
to LD Programs in Elementary and Secondary
Schools Throughout the United States

SCHOOLS OF THE NORTHEAST

SCHOOLS OF THE SOUTHEAST

SCHOOLS OF THE MIDWEST

SCHOOLS OF THE FAR WEST

Introduction

Learning disabilities constitute a new field of study. Like ecology and cybernetics, the topic is one of recent origin. Much has been learned; much is yet to be discovered. As professionals in the fields of education, medicine and the social sciences have gained insights into the LD phenomenon, the lay public has reaped benefits. Children of average or above average intelligence who have perceptual or developmental abnormalities and have been unable to succeed in conventional school programs have begun to receive the special help they need. No guide or handbook exists, however, which delineates for either laymen or professionals the extent of practical schooling alternatives available to the school-age LD child.

Raegene Pernecke and I set out to rectify this situation by researching, writing and independently publishing a book on the subject. We knew there was a need for a work of this kind and we felt our personal and professional backgrounds gave us a vantage point that was both unique and usable. We have no vested interest in any one system or philosophy, even though we have studied, taught and advised in both the private and public school sectors. During the course of our work in the educational field, we have confronted the enigma of LD; we were intrigued, but also frustrated and disturbed, by the mystery and heartbreak we encountered.

As teachers, businesswomen and mothers, we both had known young people whose notably impaired learning potential prevented them from functioning effectively in the classroom, marketplace or home. We both have been present at stormy sessions where distraught parents besieged implacable educators for help while an unhappy youngster fidgeted nearby, awaiting some new pronouncement of doom. We each had worked with students who didn't, wouldn't or couldn't learn no matter how hard we tried to teach them. Mrs. Pernecke, an educator with a Master's degree in Special Education and Psychology and twenty years' teaching experience in a major metropolitan school district, has seen students advance two or three grade levels after several months of individualized instruction. I have seen school failures and dropouts go on to become Phi Beta Kappas. These academic turnarounds were thrilling but puzzling.

13

My introduction to the LD field occurred through an intimate relationship with two children and their families. This boy and girl matured differently from their older siblings. One could not read, the other could not concentrate; they failed in school. Their parents' difficult, expensive, but eventually successful, search for a solution to these children's learning problems first acquainted me with the lack of practical information regarding appropriate LD schooling placement. We, the authors, hope our book will help address this void, for we are concerned with the welfare of LD children everywhere.

The two children who initially inspired this book are now in their teens. Since their birth tremendous progress has been made in the diagnosis and remediation of learning disabilities. Federal legislation has mandated the nationwide provision of appropriate education for handicapped children of all types. LD children who meet the local or state eligibility requirements thus receive many publicly provided special services that were previously unavailable. Because they can be more flexible in their approach and more selective in their admissions, many private programs offer an appealing alternative.

But the national LD bandwagon is slowing down. Those who promulgated the entitlements of Public Law 94-142 promised more than could reasonably be delivered given the nascent art of special education and the state of the country's economy. Budgets for public education have been pinched and cut by declining enrollments, reduced state revenues and political pressures to fund other governmental services. Many taxpayers decry the monies "thrown" at special education and point out that only partial improvement has occurred in the academic achievements of the recipients of this costly instruction. Authorities in the field have reached no consensus on definition, causation, diagnosis, treatment or prognosis. None other than Samuel Kirk, the noted educator who pioneered psycholinguistic diagnostic testing for learning disabilities, declared in 1983, "The field is in a mess."

Understandably the concerned layman is confused. Gains of the past two decades may be irretrievably lost. Knowledge needs to be consolidated, and a fresh sense of direction provided so that productive work may continue. *Schooling for the Learning Disabled*, which includes *A Selective Guide to LD Programs in Elementary and Secondary Schools Throughout the United States*, attempts to bring together in succinct, layman's terms the relevant information that has formed the basis of contemporary judgments and developments in the field.

One currently used definition of learning disabilities which few authorities consider adequate states that LD is a "disorder in one or more of the basic psychological processes involved in understanding or in using language, spoken or written, which may manifest itself in an imperfect ability to listen, think, speak, read, write, spell or to do mathematical calculations." (*Federal Register*, 1977) Estimates of the size of the learning disabled population vary from 1 to 35 percent; determining the extent of LD depends on which definition is used.

Chance determines which chromosomes are joined at the time of conception, as well as the rate and nature of the neurological development that occurs as an infant grows toward intellectual maturity. Prenatal and postnatal trauma or "insults" to the brain, plus an individual's mental health, may temporarily or permanently impede later development. Learning abnormalities in an otherwise healthy, intelligent child may indicate the existence of one or more potentially disabling conditions. When this symptomatic behavior interferes significantly with "normal" learning, such as would be expected in a regular elementary or secondary school, a syndrome may be found to exist. This syndrome is what we mean by learning disabilities or LD. According to our definition, the LD onus shifts from the child to the school. What appears to be wrong may be better under other conditions.

Initially, we limited the scope of our investigation and book to those LD students whose IQ was average or above and whose disorder was neither primarily emotional nor the result of cultural deprivation. Gatekeeping was difficult, however. Toward the end of our study we allowed ourselves more leeway than at the start. Thus, *Schooling for the Learning Disabled* is about and for those whose learning disabilities are severe as well as mild, specific as well as general.

Three general categories of learning disabilities were identified: the first included those children with mild to moderate disorders who could learn if their early educational environment were appropriately sensitive to their needs; the second included those with mild disorders whose earlier educational environment had been inappropriate, whose academic foundations were therefore faulty and whose problems were usually compounded by emotional or behavioral disorders; the third and final category included those with severe receptive, processing or expressive disorders who required a special environment in order to succeed. An example of the first category might be Jackie, who needed a transition class between kindergarten and first grade, as well as special help from a reading specialist. Jamey is an example of the second; he was hyperactive and easily frustrated by his reading and writing assignments in the primary grades, and by the time he was in junior high he had few friends and could not read above a third grade level. Pat had very poor physical coordination, could not remember things said, lacked organizational ability and could not benefit from conventional basic instruction. These three categories require slightly different instructional emphases: developmental help (extra support), correctional help (reeducation) and remediation. Depending on the child and the education received at critical learning junctures, he could move from one category to another and/or outgrow the LD label. The hope of the authors of *Schooling for the Learning Disabled* is that this book will assist parents and others to know where a particular child fits on the aforementioned continuum and which type of instruction is most appropriate.

The last section of this book contains descriptions of 50 school programs for LD students. These are a cross section of good schools; they are not necessarily the best, for other programs deserve inclusion if all the "best" are to be described. Readers are advised to review both sections of this book, so that they may understand how and why the selection process occurred as it did.

Profits accruing from the sale of this book will be used to publish a second edition which will contain an expanded *Guide* section and an updated version of the school descriptions presented in this edition.

Sara M. Schreiner

CHAPTER I

Historical Background

General Features of Contemporary
American Public Education

The modern American school system is charged with educating all youth in this country until they reach at least the age of 16. Every state and local school system must wrestle separately with decisions as to how this will be done. Most Americans take this extraordinary mandate rather for granted, relying on elected officials to ensure that the younger generation is taught what it needs to know. These decision-making boards tend to concentrate on fiscal matters and leave the substantive issues to school personnel. The trend is to fall back on traditional curricular concepts and practices remembered from childhood days. But pressure groups, demographic shifts and governmental agencies frequently force major changes.

The best schools have leaders who can interpret the significance of contemporary events, relate these to the past and convince those affected to react appropriately. Without such leadership, obsolescence, closure, chaos or mediocrity often enues. School systems that prepared in advance for the civil rights legislation of the 60s and the special education rulings of the 70s continued to provide quality education to the majority of students enrolled in their districts. But many school communities have had to forego plans and objectives in order to deal with issues such as budget deficits, enrollment changes, declining test scores, student apathy, juvenile felonies and organizational squabbling. Of necessity, schools adapt and adjust to social change, but they must do so in a farsighted, coherent, constructive fashion if today's youth are to be equipped to cope with tomorrow's problems.

The buzz phrases of the early 80s in the education field have included "learning disabilities," "mainstreaming" and "minimal competency." These are likely to be replaced soon by terms such as "high tech," "tuition tax credits" and the "New Basics." Those concerned with the complex issue of learning disabilities are worried that the legitimate needs of LD students may take a back seat in the haste to reform the educational system. Educators currently are busy trying to placate critics who demand to know what's so special about special education.

One way to counter the critics is for LD children's advocates to be well informed. Parents and educators need to stay informed, lest what is viewed as expensive, preferential treatment for LD students be abolished altogether in the nation's public schools. Besides keeping up with the latest research, advocates need to know about the history of learning disabilities *per se* and of formalized learning in general. This background information carries with it the sanction of the ages, for LD — properly understood — is as old as the human race. Specific learning disabilities are new in that science has just begun to recognize them. They cannot be dismissed as of fleeting import, however, for inadequately or improperly treated LD youth contribute disproportionately to the rising number of suicides, crime and unemployment among the youth population. All Americans need to apply their full intelligence in coping with the world's problems. All need to be able to speak, listen, read, write, reason and do mathematical calculations. These abilities are now basic to survival.

1952 — 1983

Before scanning the panorama of human history for insights into LD, it is wise to look at the emergence of this phenomenon over the past 30 years. Try imagining life in the mid-50s. Dwight Eisenhower was President, Senator McCarthy made a cult of political nondeviance, normalcy was the rule. Dumbies and brains didn't fit easily into the established order, but people kept quiet about whatever problems these nonconformists had.

Then, on October 19, 1957, the Russians launched their *Sputnik* satellite. The mood of America changed almost overnight. Suddenly the public wanted to overhaul the educational system to produce scientists and technicians capable of countering the Soviet achievements in outer space. Classroom teachers everywhere felt the pressure to bear down on students and to improve their performance.

At about the same time, the news media were spreading the word about laboratory and clinical findings regarding the human brain. Parents were already acquainted with child psychology, thanks to the popularized works of Drs. Arnold Gesell and Benjamin Spock. It appeared that unless children began schooling at an earlier age their intellectual growth would be stunted. Tax-supported Head Start programs and private, experimental nursery schools cropped up across the United States. Parents demanded a voice in determining what was best for their children; hitherto school authorities had been thought to know best.

Sputnik and Spock wrought major changes in the purposes and format of schools. But, lo, many a Johnny could not read! Disgruntled parents received little sympathy from educators bent on pleasing the tax-paying majority who wanted demonstrably impressive achievements from students. An era of progressivism was under way. Basic methods that emphasized phonics, drill, homework, standards and universal values were out. Methodology was in. Relevance was what mattered. Dismay turned to indignation as parents of the nonreaders, armed with facts about perceptual handicaps, minimal brain dysfunction, developmental aphasia, dyslexia, hyperactivity, etc., nagged school officials for structure, discipline and personalized attention in their children's classrooms. These parents felt that children with hidden handicaps were just as entitled to special education as were deaf, blind, retarded and physically handicapped youngsters. Parents formed groups or started their own schools in hopes of reducing the ever-mounting frustration they and their children were experiencing.

In 1963, representatives from these groups met in Chicago to coordinate their efforts. The term *learning disability* was adopted as the phrase best describing the nature of their children's problems; it was thought that the mode of teaching directly affected the quality of learning. A national network-type organization was formed under the name of the Association for Children with Learning Disabilities (ACLD). Thus, from the outset LD was a generic term. Efforts to narrow the definition and to avoid its indiscriminate use have been unsuccessful. Meanwhile, ACLD's advocacy of the rights and needs of learning disabled students led to their inclusion in entitlement legislation passed by Congress in 1975. According to Public Law 94-142, the Education for All Handicapped Children Act, parents could rightfully expect that their LD child would get a free, appropriate public education, that he/she would be educated to the maximum extent possible with nonhandicapped children in what was called a "least restrictive environment" and that the school would document the elements of this appropriate education.

This legislation and subsequent regulations regarding special education provided services to children who were behaviorally disordered, emotionally disturbed and mentally retarded (the educable and trainable mentally handicapped), as well as the learning disabled. School systems that had not already done so complied with the law, since the 1954 Brown decision had established the right of the Federal government to overrule the states' wishes whenever students were denied their constitutionally guaranteed rights to fair and equal treatment. Self-contained classrooms and resource rooms were created, teachers certified in special education were added to staffs, and ways were devised to shift handicapped youngsters in and out of regular classes so that the intent of the law might be upheld. Many elementary schools modified their grouping and scheduling practices effectively so that good, individual remediation could be subtly and promptly incorporated into a youngster's program. Children who otherwise might have been shunted aside progressed in close-to-normal fashion.

Junior and senior high schools had to deal with more severe, less amenable problems for, by the time students approached puberty with unresolved learning difficulties, acute emotional and behavioral disturbances often accompanied the specific learning disability or developmental delay. Parental expectations often played an important part—both negatively and positively—in the affective response children made to earlier academic failures. Negative attitudes were not easily changed. The additional stigma of being grouped with a bunch of "retards and burnouts" at a time when peer pressure is greatest, i.e., in adolescence, made and makes LD remediation at the high school level even more problematic. Handicapped children may look and act "different." Because most are aware they are different and therefore not quite "with it," they act out and "scapegoat" one another when together. Youngsters want not to be grouped apart, and when faced with an assignment to a special education resource room, they will resist. Being in a multicategorical resource room in a comprehensive high school may mean that the child's self-esteem, learning habits, basic skills and motivation become worse, even though in the better schools there usually is on hand a host of specially trained support service personnel who tutor, test, counsel, diagnose and serve as liaison with the LD student's regular teachers. Being in the mainstream is often the only thing that matters. A sizable number of LD students are substantially helped through the aforementioned services. If any readers of these remarks were to visit public school LD programs, they might find a cross categorical resource area in a suburban Chicago school bustling with upbeat kids, purposeful activity and a "turned-on" staff. They might also visit special education departments that had a depressingly different atmosphere. The authors experienced both.

Due process hearings are on the increase, especially at the secondary level, as parents react to the school's failure to accomplish the goals of their child's individual educational program. Civil suits are being filed against many districts for failing to educate individual LD children. Further, because of burgeoning requests for LD placement, eligibility requirements have been made stiffer. State and local formulas often specify that a child be functioning at about two grade levels below his expected performance level before he/she may receive special services. This means that many students who might be helped by early intervention must wait until their problems become worse and less manageable. Administrators of the nation's schools, particularly in the urban and suburban areas, are rethinking the whole special education situation. Ideally, their thoughts will lead to such improvement in the quality of the curriculum and instruction that the unique personalities, needs and learning styles of each student may be accommodated within a regular classroom setting. But a new wrinkle has been added of late, and this concern may take precedence over any attempt to straighten out the mess in special education.

The Immediate Danger

In the spring of 1983, the National Commission of Excellence in Education issued a report titled, "A Nation at Risk,"which stated that academic expectations and achievements had so declined in the 26 years since Sputnik that more than 13 percent, for instance, of the nation's 17-year-olds were functionally illiterate. The knowledge explosion of this century has transformed society; what was once an industrial society is now a postindustrial one in which the processing and the producing of information account for more than 60 percent of the jobs available. Citizens living in this "information age ... who do not possess the levels of skill, literacy and training essential to this new era will be effectively disenfranchised." The report states that "the unimaginable of a generation ago has begun to occur"; other world competitors are "matching and surpassing our education attainments." "Part of what is at risk is the promise first made on this continent: All, regardless of race or class or economic status, are entitled to a fair chance and to the tools for developing their individual powers of mind and spirit to the utmost." Among "the nation's youth who are most at risk" are "the handicapped." By implication, this means the learning disabled. School authorities will have to decide which programs will be scrapped and which will be beefed up. Inasmuch as there is not enough money in school coffers to do everything the government requires, cost effectiveness will be the governing principle. As public interest and attention shift away from learning disabilities, what can advocates do to keep momentum going? Is it in the best interests of this society to continue to protect the legitimate needs of youngsters who otherwise would be dysfunctional?

21

Schooling and Learning Since the Dawn of History

All life is an adaptation to nature. Nature, in turn, is kindest to those organisms that possess the intelligence and adaptive capability to respond adroitly to her presence and power. Mankind has enjoyed nature's favor. It has taken more than 500 million years of successive mutations for animal life to reach the state where it can understand itself. Only man has been so endowed, for atop his spinal column rests a brain that enables him to respond consciously in novel ways to the stimuli of his natural environment. Like his predecessors, the apes, man can react reflexively, instinctively and intuitively; he can learn conditioned responses and imitate behavior. But he can also perceive abstract relationships. He has the neural matter to discern connections between his sensory experiences. He can see the sun and feel its warmth and then objectify this dual sensation and signify its essence by means of some symbolic act—either a gesture, a guttural sound or the designation of some object or mark. Man can name things. He can assign words to objects, events and processes. He can know and communicate through language the secrets of nature.

Sign language was undoubtedly the first kind of symbolic expression. Speech or oral language must have come next, followed by writing or graphic communication. By the time man was drawing animal pictures in caves 50,000 years ago, he may have had between 100 and 500 words in his vocabulary. The unique value of these arbitrary vocal sounds was that the clan or group now had a communicable core of understanding. Cooperation and differentiated responsibility could begin to occur in the ways the group organized itself to combat threats to its survival.

At first, words were not arranged in sentences; relationships between words were conveyed by intonation, inflection or bodily gesture. The earliest evidence of a comprehensive spoken language system dates back only 7,000 years. The Aryan or Indo-European tongue and the people who used it seem to have predominated over a large geographic area. Eight other totally different tongues must have coexisted during the next 2,000 years, for anthropologists and philologists have found that many separate families of root words and corresponding verbal and grammatical forms that exist today relate to prehistoric clusters of people and culture. So different are these tongues that the peoples speaking them were and still are conditioned thereby to think and act differently. Words, which represent ideas, have a life of their own. So long as a people's linguistically based thoughts and actions enabled them to adapt successfully to their environment, they and their way of life survived. Nature tended to preserve the speech patterning or programming capabilities of these people's brains, in the same way that computer "brains" are preprogrammed to speak different languages, e.g., BASIC, PASCAL and COBOL. It is no wonder that a polyglot nation, such as the United States, in which genetically different racial and cultural strains have met through social and sexual intercourse would find it difficult to learn or teach in any uniform way the intricacies and subtleties of the English language. The Japanese, whose language does not contain the *L* phoneme, have great difficulty learning to pronounce this sound after a certain age. Non-Germans may learn to decode words such as *Weltanschauung* but may never appreciate the connotative meaning. Similarly, Einstein, who manifested the symptoms of the learning disabled when young, could not explain his theory of relativity in words, although he thought he could play it on the violin. A youngster may inherit insufficiently strong auditory, speech or visual transmission channels to handle readily certain phonemes, morphemes or concepts.

Nevertheless, the child goes off to school at a very young age and is expected to imprint linguistic input automatically, even though his immature nervous system may not be designed to decode or encode it easily. New untried pathways must be developed. People need compelling reasons to start charting and following a new course. On the one hand, the human being instinctively tries to conserve energy; inertia is a powerful, safeguarding force, and minds usually take the paths of least resistance. On the other hand, man seems destined and driven to survive by the strength of his wits and his relatedness to his world and fellow creatures. This inner drive is what has led to advances in civilization. The situation is analogous to that of a traveler who comes to a river and finds the bridge unsafe or otherwise impassable; he must find a new way to cross the river — either by fixing the bridge or by swimming or by using a boat or by finding a shallower spot — or else turn back.

Schools arrived late on the scene of history. The right — or requirement — to attend had an even later debut. The need for schools arose when it was no longer sufficient for the young just to copy the actions and thought patterns of adults. Language had created a body of knowledge, access to which was only fully gained through the acquisition of linguistic skills. Writing, in particular, allowed the accumulation and preservation of laws, literature, prescriptions and commercial transactions beyond the duration of individual memory.

Writing — and hence reading — were required to be known by some segment of the society. Those chosen by the priests and ruling chieftains to learn to write were given formal instruction. The other youth were informally taught the group folkways and practices considered essential for communal existence and survival. Boys often were apprenticed; girls were expected to learn domestic arts from older women. It would be surprising if the earliest schools had encouraged independent exercise of the mind, for rigid conformity to the group ethos kept internal conflict to a minimum. Even so, those chosen for initiation into the ranks of the ruling elite received training not only in writing, but also in the arts of oratory, medicine, magic, astronomy, warfare, and, ultimately, grammar and logic.

By the 12th century B.C., these arts had yielded abundant fruit. The epics of Homer are the account of an heroic and worldly race whose deeds and devotion to duty fired the imagination of the fledgling Greek city states. This fostered the creation of a spirit of mind that made Greece the school of Hellas and the ideal of Western civilizations. In Athens, the leisurely pursuit of knowledge for its own sake by all freemen of the polis was a mode of living. Defeat in war meant the end of Athenian democracy and of its humanistic institutions. Governments ever since have been trying to balance individualism with the maintenance of public welfare.

The Romans borrowed Greek ideas, but they opted for law and order, only to find in the fifth century A.D., that the governed had too little allegiance to the state to withstand the encroachments of barbarian hordes from the North. The schools that emerged in Europe after Charlemagne's time were for the instruction of the faithful in the practices and dogma of the Christian church. Children of the aristocracy were enabled to prepare to enter one of the three learned professions — Law, Medicine or Theology — and to learn something of science. But, even with the rise of a middle class, few youth had formal schooling. Class distinctions based upon educational opportunities underlie much of European history. The practices of St. Ignatius of Loyola and of John Calvin and the theories of philosophers such as John Locke and Jean Jacques Rousseau went against the stratified grain of the Continent.

When the dissidents, dispossessed and disenfranchised of the Old World came to the shores of the New World they sought a form of liberty and security different from that which they had left behind. Still it took at least a century before rival beliefs could coalesce enough to begin building state-supported systems of education. Up until the early 20th century most citizens in America could barely write their name. The United States' transition from an agrarian society to an industrial one, its institution of universal suffrage, and its attraction of vast numbers of immigrants required a common ground of acculturation. States took over the general administration and supervision of the tax-supported schools within their boundaries. The standardization process has now reached the point where the granting or withholding of Federal funds can ensure state conformity to regional or national mandates. *E pluribus unum.* The question of "liberty and justice for all" is being answered anew in the laboratories of the schools.

24

The Origin of the LD Concept

Probably LD youngsters only surfaced in times past when societal pressures required that all perform in exacting ways. When life is slow and its rhythms unimperiled, individuals can adjust at their leisure. In times of rapid change, force prevails. In perilous times throughout the ancient world children of feeble mind or body frequently were destroyed or abandoned soon after birth. Tales are told of how societies used to punish their recalcitrants and nonconformists by flogging, ostracizing, disinheriting or mocking them. Some were viewed as possessed by devils that had to be exorcized. Some were burned as heretics. Some simply disappeared. Typical of the attitude of many is Montaigne's comment regarding what to do if a boy refused to learn or was proved incapable of it: ". . . his tutor should strangle him, if there are no witnesses, or else he should be apprenticed to a pastry cook in some good town." Mankind has not been very humane to its geniuses, either. Anyone who balked or rebelled when forced to perform in group-prescribed ways had rough going. The ones who were clumsy, absent-minded, gauche, antisocial, reticent or otherwise dumb-appearing are in the closets of history.

Through the centuries, theories have been postulated to explain physicial and mental abnormalities, but it was not until the late 1800s and thereafter that disabling learning conditions and their correction received attention.

In Britain, three physicians noted that some of their patients who had been treated for emotional problems in reality were suffering from an inability to read. Earlier, a Frenchman, Broca, had discovered during an autopsy a connection between speech impairment and localized left hemisphere brain damage. A German had described a "word-blindness" condition. Surgeons during World War I began to recognize that communication problems arising from brain lesions could be alleviated by educational rehabilitation. After systematic testing, Alfred Binet devised a means to measure human intelligence. The American educator, John Dewey, argued convincingly that learning occurs through doing, that educators should base instruction on psychological and sociological principles and that students' unique learning strengths and capacities should be developed.

Samuel Orton, a neuropathologist well aware of these earlier developments, recognized that reading problems in a child of normal intelligence often were associated with mixed dominance between the right and left sides of the body and brain. Between 1927 and 1936, he experimented with and treated children with language disorders. With Anna Gillingham and Bessie Stillman, he refined these ideas and developed a teaching method based on phonics instruction rather than a sight word approach to reading.

Simultaneously, philosophers were evincing considerable interest in the ideas of an Austrian, Ludwig Wittgenstein, who suggested that the real problems of logic and reason were ones of linguistics. Thereafter, scholars began feuding as to whether language should be studied and taught in a structural way or as transformational grammar. World War II and the introduction of rapid aural/oral means of teaching foreign languages prompted an end to traditional, outmoded rote grammar instruction.

The 20th century was intrigued—rightfully—by new insights into the organic and functional aspects of the human brain. Educators became aware that motor development and learnings were prerequisite to perception and cognition. Pathfinders such as Alfred Strauss, Laura Lehtinen Rogan, Newell Kephart and William Cruikschanck worked to improve individual perceptual organization through multisensory techniques. Educators also found that children need to succeed in their early school situations if they are not to become emotionally unstable and are not to hate or fear school. The importance of positive feedback was acknowledged, along with the need for structure. Science discovered that certain medications can arrest severe psychotic and emotional problems, as well as effect a person's ability to concentrate and function normally. The acknowledgment of the electrochemical basis for brain functioning profoundly redirected the emphases of many teacher-training institutions toward a more mechanistic orientation. The very recent acceptance of the value of computers in expediting the acquisition of skills and knowledge through the instant feedback principle comes at a time when there is a craze to denigrate teaching as a profession and also when the family unit is undergoing major disruption.

Education as a fundamental basis for progress, self-fulfillment and societal preservation needs enlightened proponents. The concept of learning disabilities may make or break the world. The convergence of vital new understandings regarding genetics, linguistics, behavior, anthropology, ethics, economics, political science and inner and outer space along with the mandates of special education in the 1980s underscore the imminence of revolutionary social change. LD is not alone at the crossroads.

The question remains to be answered: "Is it in the best interests of this society to continue to protect the legitimate needs of youngsters who otherwise would be dysfunctional?"

ꬶꬶꬶ

The authors believe that individual differences are assets. Furthermore, the mainstream is made of different individuals, each with his or her own need, style, gift and potential contribution. The real danger in 1984 and this world is that the collective and the mass will unwittingly destroy individuality, creativity and perhaps initiative and human dignity. Providing special educational opportunities for those who do not learn in a "normal" way is not an act of charity, but an investment in the well-being of all of society. Norms exist only in the field of statistics. Realistically, no human being is normal. The money being spent for special education is seed money. Ultimately, special education may be available to everyone.

CHAPTER II

Learning and
Human Development

Learning disabled children can achieve academic success. Their mental capacity is such that given the proper training at the proper time and an appropriately supportive home environment, most LD youngsters will develop the confidence and skills to lead happy, productive lives. Some may go on to become our world's pathfinders; Leonardo da Vinci, Thomas Edison, Albert Einstein and Winston Churchill were all divergent thinkers whose early academic and social experiences approximated those of LD youth.

Scientific progress during the past 50 years has enabled researchers and special educators to begin fathoming the mysteries of the mind and to adapt instructional practices to different modes of learning. Those providing remediation to LD youngsters have actually led the way to the frontiers of human understanding by showing how the brain can work to its best advantage, how human potential may be more effectively realized, and how blocks in the central nervous system may be bypassed or rendered less handicapping.

Current views on the causes, or etiology, of learning disabilities are conflicting. To clarify these issues and to appreciate better how the brain develops and functions, the authors asked Dr. Frank H. Mayfield, a distinguished neurosurgeon and educator with 50 years of clinical and research experience in the neural sciences, for insight. His comments follow:

The human brain is a very complex organ; it is the seat of the soul, the secreter of emotions and thoughts, the hiding place of fear. The child who appears normal but who cannot keep pace with his peers in school is frightened. Fear of the unknown and of social failure are the cruelest of human tortures. The child's problems in school are aggravated by the parents' anxiety and fear.

Scientists of necessity develop a special language to record their findings and opinions. This language is understood and appropriately used by fellow workers. The writer who undertakes to translate these findings into laymen's terms has a profound responsibility. Parents, through fear, are highly vulnerable to peaks of hope and pits of depression in relation to the progress of their offspring. I am, therefore, deeply concerned about this as I undertake to address the fundamental question of the development of the brain in relation to the learning process.

Much is known of the anatomy (architecture), the physiology (function) and disease (pathology) of the brain. This knowledge has been gained over the centuries by carefully comparing the disability of patients with known disease, such as tumor, stroke or injury, with findings at the operating table and at autopsy. To this knowledge, technical developments have recently added new and exciting insights into the inner structure, the chemistry and the electricity of the brain.

Educators and behavioral scientists meanwhile have been gathering and analyzing data about the learning experience. Already much is known about the classification of learning disorders and the placement of children once the problem is suspected. The potential for good in all these areas of research is unlimited; yet it is rare to find a specific, comprehensive diagnostic answer in the individual case.

As Emerson said, "Each of us is a new creation in nature; no two of us are alike." The human has not been cloned. Just as we differ in facial features, color and temperament, so do our brains differ. It should surprise no one, therefore, that we learn differently.

When the sperm and ovum meet and fuse, all the genetic material for one human being is there. This coded material determines how many neurons (nerve cells) each of us will have (billions, perhaps trillions). It also determines certain instincts or emotions that will be used to distinguish between pleasurable experiences, such as food, sex and love, and unpleasurable experiences, such as pain, anger, fear and horror. These instincts are essential to survival. They are present in every animal species from the lizard to the mammal to the human.

The single-cell embryo grows rapidly by dividing. Very quickly the workload is divided into three parts: one group of cells forms the entire digestive system; another builds the skeleton, muscles and ligaments; the third forms the skin and the nervous system (brain, spinal cord, peripheral nerves). Those cells committed to form the nervous system quickly gather themselves into a tube (neural tube). Those portions of the neural tube destined to form the brain multiply with great speed. Most of them migrate or are pushed to the surface to form the cortex (gray matter). Once the genetically predetermined quantity of neurons has been produced and these cells have reached their destination, they can no longer multiply. They tend to take up special positions in the brain and thereafter to perform special functions.

The growth of the brain is so rapid that it forces the skull and scalp to expand before it. But nature, in what Cannon has called "the wisdom of the body," has the skull resist the growth until it can partition the brain case into several parts. Otherwise the heavy brain (nine pounds) would be destroyed by the ordinary movements of living. The partitions function then like an egg crate or bulkhead of a ship and semicompartmentalize the work. The principal partition runs from front to back through the brain case and partially divides the brain into two halves called hemispheres. These are, in turn, divided into lobes (sections). A large mass of white fibers (axons) called the *corpus* (body) *callosum* (hard) connects the two hemispheres. The axons transmit messages from one side of the brain to the other.

This transmission is essential to coordinated function. For example, if one picks up a signal in the left hand that requires response by the right hand, the signal goes to the right cortex for processing and is then sent to the left cortex for action. We do know that the function of speech is located in the left side of the brain in most right-handed individuals. This location varies substantially if the individual is left-handed or ambidextrous.

Much is being written now about the subject of the dominance of one hemisphere or the other. The studies in this regard are important, but as yet the applications have little practical value to the individual case.

During the growth of the cortex (data processing) little nests of cells remain lower down in the brain (brain stem) to serve such basic functions of life as breathing, nutrition and blood circulation. The memory function is located in the medial (near the middle) side of the temporal lobe and is closely connected with all of the nests of cells (basal ganglia) that serve the basic functions of life. This memory center carries the instinctual memories necessary for survival. Thereafter, throughout the living experience, new memories are recorded as pleasant or unpleasant.

These substations in the brain are connected by a ringlike structure called the lymbic system, which regulates automatic survival functions. All neurons of the cortex are connected therefore with one another. Another connecting system in the brain, the reticular (network) activating system, determines whether we wake or sleep. These structures and systems at the base of the brain act like booster stations and transformers. They generate two classes of neurotransmitters: one of them makes us alert and awake; the other makes us drowsy and we fall asleep. In street parlance these are "uppers" and "downers." These chemical neurotransmitters are consumed in the process of brain function.

The neurons of the cortex which process data are very delicate. They cannot survive without oxygen for more than a few moments, and they are vulnerable even to changes in temperature. They depend on another group of cells called glia. These cells fit around each neuron like glue and provide nutrition. The glial cells grow very slowly.

The development of motor and sensory skills must wait in each individual until the glia can provide the neuron with the food supply system it needs to function. It is this process we watch in the growing child. The process continues until at least the age of 4 years and explains why a child's intellectual development doesn't always keep pace with the obvious brain growth.

If the cortex can be accepted as the data processor of our human computer system and the temporal lobes as our data bank, then the special anatomical senses of vision, hearing, taste and smell along with the important tactile and kinesthetic sensations should be considered as the programmers. Sensory impressions that receive attention and those which are organized into a pattern of associations are transferred from the short-term memory area to the long-term temporal storage area behind the frontal lobes.

The highly sensitive and complex organ that is our human brain must make its way into a hostile world through the valley of the shadow of birth. The world is bristling with danger such as toxic microbes, malnutrition and injuries. If we can accept the premise that one begins genetically with a differing number of neurons and circuits and that some of these circuits may not survive birth and infancy, it will be obvious that some will begin the learning experience with relative handicaps. If the learning handicap is widespread and associated with injuries to other parts of the brain, it is rarely overlooked. More subtle impairments, such as those that interfere with the ability to decode or translate a written word into understandable language, impose a major problem. They are difficult to identify because the child tends to divert attention from the defect by behaving inappropriately.

The child who is hyperactive, the one who has an overly brief attention span and the child who misbehaves among his peers without reason should lead parents and teachers to suspect a learning disability. A study should be carried out by those capable of detecting and identifying defects of the learning system. Punishment or disciplinary action for not trying hard enough usually makes the problem worse. When punishment becomes associated with learning, the child equates the effort to learn with recalled painful or unpleasant experiences.

The brain functions normally by rejecting all signals that are not useful to it at the moment; we call this "concentration." The cool athlete or the star performer or the master surgeon is able, as a rule, to reject the consequences of failure and therefore to perform without inhibition. The learning disabled child is not only unable to concentrate easily; often when he does he perseverates.

When diagnostic testing reveals an area of impairment, it is usually possible for skilled and sensitive teachers to find ways to bypass the defect. One cannot always precisely identify those circuits that are not functioning; but one can teach the child by trial, error and love to use the circuits that do work. Thus the child can begin to enjoy the learning experience. This process requires of teachers and parents alike absolute commitment and infinite patience.

When the fear of failure is replaced by self-esteem and the neurotransmitter of love, instead of hate, is drawn from the memory bank, the child may be said to be receiving appropriate education. Helen Keller, born deaf and blind, was lonely and bitter until a teacher so nurtured her with love that she overcame her defects and became one of the world's great philosophers. "Miracles" such as this are attributable to the soul's tenacity and superb teaching; this match-up takes place in countless classrooms throughout the country.

As Dr. Mayfield has suggested, the subconscious will influences the soul with its inner drive and restraints and animates human behavior and thus learning. When a child wants to do or learn something, he/she will put forth effort; he/she will consciously choose to attend and respond to stimuli. A newborn's first instinctive, air-hungry cry usually elicits a need-satisfying response from the external environment; this cry tends to be repeated whenever needs arise. The growing child gradually acquires ego strength and self-awareness through interaction with and feedback from the world about him/her. His/her self perception will affect the confidence with which he/she ventures into new, risky encounters. The child will seek to imitate and please those upon whom he/she depends for physical nurture and positive affective rewards. If efforts to copy and please are unsuccessful, they will be abandoned. Behavioral psychologists call these "conditioned responses." The behaviorists undergird many of the teaching strategies used in LD classrooms and schools.

People change for several basic reasons: (1) change is imposed from without, as with an injury; (2) it is genetically determined, as with growth and maturation; (3) the perception of reality is altered by experience, as with a political reorientation of values and (4) change is self-imposed, as with the decision to diet or study. Parents and educators incorporate all four modification modes in training children. They may punish a child, integrate adult expectations with the emerging, developing wants of the child, structure the child's environment in such a way that certain habits of mind are inculcated and reinforce positive child-initiated decisions.

The problem for parents and teachers of learning disabled students is that LD students react atypically to most learning situations. These children interfere with lesson plans, classroom routines and schedules. Negative feedback within many large groups reduces their initiative and may cause LD students to retreat from interaction with classmates or to resort to disruptive attention-getting devices. An LD child will seek the company of those who make him feel good. Parents and peers may not approve of these companions, and often a vicious cycle of acceptance and rejection plummets the child totally out of the social mainstream.

The increasing sophistication of psychoeducational testing has led to better diagnoses, good individual instructional planning and exciting new curricular materials. These capitalize on a student's strengths and skirt his weaknesses until a pattern of success has been established. Inherent in these new ideas, materials and techniques is the concept that a student not move on to more difficult work until earlier, prerequisite tasks are accomplished. The trick is to make the content age-appropriate and not to bore the student by excessive repetition.

Standing precedes the act of walking. Before a child can walk, he must have sufficient balance, strength and agility to remain erect on two feet. The time required to master any basic skill varies from child to child. This time interval is influenced by cognitive readiness, emotional attitudes and the quality of instruction given. Once an underlying concept or skill is mastered, the learning rate may speed up considerably. Children who cannot yet accurately perceive the difference between curves and angles or a *hiss* and a *shhh* cannot differentiate between oral and written symbols and thus learn to read. Children whose memory experiences and whose sense of time and space are fragmented, disorganized or distorted cannot make much sense of incoming verbal data. Perception, whether of sounds, images, patterns, sequences, space, time, directions or behavioral cues, is not knowledge; it is the precursor to knowledge. When students are methodically helped to correct or allow for faulty perceptions, step by step, page by page, they can then proceed to more abstract learning. This sequential process of going from the simple to the complex, the concrete to the abstract, is the basis of most schooling.

Norm-referenced testing is the usual and most convenient but not necessarily the most appropriate way to ensure that learning tasks have been accomplished. This testing can determine if most students in a class have understood what was taught. However, the purpose is to discriminate between people, to spread them out on a curve in such a way as to suggest who has mastered certain content. In the typical classroom there often is not a true correspondence between what is taught and what is tested. Some students will score higher than the norm (or average) and others will not. Usually a small percentage will receive an A or 100 percent; another small percentage will fail. The latter group usually is given a chance to retake the test and improve on the original grade, but the assumption is that studying harder will bring improvement. If most students understand and respond correctly on a test, the fact that some fail is not viewed as the teacher's fault, but the student's. The typical teacher doesn't have sufficient free time to work one-on-one with a student to correct mistakes and misunderstandings. Also, since good grades tend to motivate those who receive them and have the opposite effect on those who don't, rarely will the failing student become enthused about trying harder.

Except in homogeneously grouped classes, students rarely benefit equally from the same instruction, given their different learning styles, ability levels and backgrounds. If a ghetto child goes into a suburban classroom, he/she is likely to be confused by many of the references and expectations.

Most standardized achievement and intelligence quotient (IQ) testing resembles the typical norm-referenced classroom quiz and grade. But the former generally are consistent predictors of overall achievement and/or ability because they have been pretested and are based on the scores of a large and diverse testing population. The measuring devices may consist of objective norms, percentile ranks or scaled scores; a student's placement on these various "yardsticks" allows useful comparisons. When there is a major discrepancy between achievement and intelligence or verbal and performance ability, a learning disability usually is suspected.

LD students benefit most from what is called *criterion-referenced* testing. This phrase simply means that a student works on a skill until a test reveals that skill mastery has occurred. An example might be testing for the mastery of the ability to lift a particular weight a certain distance off the ground on two of three tries. The criteria are the act to be performed and the conditions under which it is to be done. Another example might be the correct spelling of 19 out of 20 words on a test of similar-sounding words. The student does not proceed to the next spelling lesson or level until he has achieved 95 percent mastery. The Individual Educational Programs (IEPs) called for in Public Law 94-142 set forth short- and long-term goals to be accomplished by the student and the teacher, as well as the means of determining whether these goals are met; criterion-referenced testing is an integral part of most of these evaluative procedures.

Learning has been referred to as the creation of programs in the brain. LD students vitally need structure and extra help in laying structurally sound "program" foundations on which to build later learning. By using small, incremental learning steps and criterion-referenced testing procedures, the student moves from success to success. The pressure is off to do something by a certain time; such pressure makes many LD students panic. But by seeing the success their efforts yield, students tend to willingly apply themselves to their prescribed learning agendas. Some curricular materials designed around these principles may be self-checked; with a teacher nearby to step in and monitor progress, modify the assignment or clarify misunderstanding, students tend to zoom along. They take to this form of instruction in the same way they respond to computer games and instruction, for in both there are instant feedback and structured progress. Computers now employ humor, creative simulations, review, drill and practice as part of their "teaching."

Data stored in the brain's short-term memory bank last less than 20 seconds; only when transferred to the permanent storage area can an idea or skill be considered learned. So repetition and memorization are part and parcel of mastery. How and whether repetitive drill is used as a teaching strategy with LD students is controversial — for the teacher, the curriculum designers and the parents. This issue confronts the question of which type of instruction is best. Besides being individualized, success-oriented and mastery-based, what should be taught an LD student and how? Should learning processes be emphasized, or academic content? Should instruction be on a group or one-to-one basis? Should the classroom atmosphere be strict or permissive? Should parents be intimately involved or not? Should rote drill be used?

Experts do not agree on the answers. There are advantages and disadvantages to any single approach.

More than a decade ago, enthusiasm for independent and individualized learning flourished. One popular model enabled students to work on a sequential, individually paced contract basis under the supervision of a teacher who both designed the student learning package and monitored progress. After trial periods in traditional public high schools, this instructional mode became dubbed the "flat tire" of secondary education. It was discovered that few teachers had the curricular and diagnostic expertise to devise manageable and appropriate learning objectives for their 100 to 150 students. Also, most students missed the synergistic give-and-take of classroom dynamics, and they tended to progress very slowly while off "doing their own thing." For certain students, this type of program was tailor-made, however.

Belonging to a group is highly prized, even by those who persistently fall into the loser category. Where several modes of teaching, grouping and testing are incorporated into a teaching situation, there are proportionally fewer consistent losers. But not all teachers can adapt themselves to different learning styles. Where team teaching is used, fewer students slip through the classroom "cracks". For the same reason, paraprofessional classroom aides are often a boon.

Among the basic types of direct instruction are the lecture, discovery/dialogue and coaching methods. One-to-one tutoring can incorporate all three. However, the skill and knowledge of the tutor are of critical importance. In either a one-to-one or a group situation, a charismatic, knowledgeable and talented instructor can accomplish wonders, but the focused attention and time on task possible in a tutorial usually bring about faster learning. Contemporary time studies have demonstrated that students at a large, comprehensive school may receive no more than 90 minutes of direct instruction during a typical week's worth of classes. Recitation is common to all three instructional modes; students respond orally to questions about material previously taught and/or studied. The effectiveness of this practice bears directly on the teacher's ability.

Because LD students do not fit a convenient mold and because the modalities (or sensory channels) and instructional techniques by which they learn most effectively differ widely, it follows that except in those schools where only students with like learning profiles are admitted the learning breakdown will occur most often in large group situations. Among dyslexics there is great diversity. Some learn best by a phonics-oriented approach; others learn best by a whole-word or linguistics approach. Individualized educational programs are invaluable at critical early points in a student's academic career. Highly specialized approaches may be required.

Among the very distinctive approaches that are not usually offered by itinerant or resource room teachers in the public schools are the Orton-Gillingham phonics approach and the Fernald method. The former involves a multisensory, step-by-step process whereby words are broken down into their phonetic components, sounds are blended, suffixes and prefixes are added to the root word and a working written vocabulary is gradually developed. The Fernald method differs in that the child picks the words to be studied, and, by systematically using all the sensory modalities, the child comes to know the word as a whole. Through a painstaking process, the sight words become committed to memory, stories are created from these and reading ensues.

The objectives of these and all other elementary reading programs are to break the code and to discover the meaning of printed symbols. Alphabetic letters, musical notes and numerical notations are all abstract symbols and require the existence of an organizing principle or ability in order that their pattern and relationship to concrete reality be perceived and retained in memory. Otherwise, they are but a jumble of isolated stimuli. Some children perceive the whole but miss the details: some perceive the details and miss the Gestalt or whole. Some comprehend through hearing but not seeing or vice versa. These individual learning and perceptual differences account for the many specialized approaches to teaching the basics.

For many years, it was thought that various motor skills were prerequisite to academic masteries and thus educators developed a host of therapeutic techniques to strengthen coordination and visual perception. The value of these approaches, from the Frosting to the Delicato to the optometric programs, has not been definitively proved. Some experts feel that the improvements noted while using these specialized approaches may be more attributable to the Hawthorne effect (by which a child gets better just because attention is paid him) than to the merits of the therapies. None can argue, however, that a healthy, fully functional body is not an asset to mental and social development. The controversy that swells today around the issues of pharmaceutical intervention, nutritional regimens and vitamins in the remediation of LD is a good indication of how far science has yet to go before full understanding is gained regarding how the brain develops and functions.

In the meanwhile, parents may be thankful that they are living in an era when so much is being done and tried to provide appropriate educational assistance to those who are different.

CHAPTER III

Procedures for Managing an LD Child's Schooling

LD children need special help—from their families, school, communities and society at large. Getting the help that's needed at the most advantageous time doesn't happen automatically. Parents must be overseers and production managers, watching over the provision of educational services. Until midway through their children's teenage years, all parents, but especially those whose children are learning disabled, have to maintain a delicate balance, neither overprotecting nor overexpecting, neither meddling nor being uninvolved. One of the hardest problems an LD parent faces may be the guilt, anger or grief felt in recognizing that his or her progeny is disabled. Children are quick to sense when they have disappointed their family. Parents should *not* blame themselves; almost all try their best to do what is right in guiding their children to productive self-fulfillment. Parents may not realize their child's learning style is markedly different from that of other children. One mother who raised twins in an identical manner did not realize until kindergarten that her son did not learn the way his sister did. Grade school was a nightmare for the boy; bedwetting, tears and stomach-aches were a nightly ordeal. The girl's school work was perfect, and she was ashamed of her brother's performance. A concerted effort by the parents enabled the son to finish college at the same time as the daughter. Such support and assistance by parents are the mainstay of successful LD remediation

Parents of LD children learn to live with uncertainty as they cope with the unpredictable ups and downs of their youngster's schooling and social adjustment. Following are some procedural benchmarks that parents may wish to consider in realistically and constructively planning the course ahead. Two mottos apply: **The sooner the better,** for the sooner a child's learning problems can be addressed, the greater the chance for remediation; and **Be prepared,** for being caught off guard wastes precious time.

Early Childhood Guidelines

- If developmental milestones are not "on time" and if the physician's wait-and-see attitude seems injudicious, seek other pediatric expertise. Early medical intervention may correct or eliminate defects; regular visits give the doctor a full picture of development; medical advice allays anxiety; early testing for neurological, visual or hearing disorders may rule out or isolate physiological causes. Good private and university or hospital-affiliated diagnostic and developmental centers are found in most urban areas.
- Get individual or family counseling if child exacerbates problems in the home; join a parents' group.
- Become knowledgeable on the subject of child development; learn how the child's school readiness in areas of motor coordination, orientation in time and space, perception of colors, sounds, textures and shapes, ability to receive, interpret and respond to verbal communication can be enhanced at home.
- Eliminate from diet foods of questionable nutritional value. Some refined and processed foods are thought to have adverse effects on LD.
- Ask physician, local school district or State Department of Education for information on early screening programs that identify handicapping conditions. Federal law provides special preschool training at public expense to those eligible.
- Establish regular routines and schedules in home; have consistent and fair disciplinary policies; spend one-on-one time with child; recognize value of structure.
- Consider enrolling child in local nursery school, especially if opportunities for socialization are few and/or parent is unable to provide creative growth experiences for child at home.

Schooling Guidelines

• Delay having child enter kindergarten or first grade if child is not ready. Notify teacher immediately if child has unusual school adjustment problems.

• A routine screening may take place in elementary school. If the child doesn't "pass" screening, school should propose further evaluation; parent must agree in writing and understand rights to full participation in process, including seeing records and reports and seeking to have these changed.

• Evalution will be by a *multidisciplinary team*, including teachers and specialists, and will involve academic testing, medical and social history, psychological evaluation, assessment of speech, language, vision and hearing.

• Ensure that child is relaxed, regarding evaluation process; anxiety can invalidate test results.

• Obtain and study one of several good layman's guides to testing.

• Review test results and study child's confidential folder for critical statements about weaknesses and strengths, learning styles, sources of these judgments and nature of recommendations; decide whether descriptions are accurate.

• Plan to be present at evaluation conference and to accept or reject assessment conclusions. If child is eligible for special education services and you agree to placement recommendations, expect to take part in designing child's Individual Education Program (IEP) which sets forth (1) present level of achievement, (2) annual goals, (3) short-term behavioral objectives to reach goal, (4) which specific special services are to be provided, (5) by whom, when and under what circumstances and (6) the means for measuring progress. Plan to sign a mutually acceptable IEP.

What Is Usually Available in the Local School?

The array of options available to most public school students, depending on eligibility, includes the following levels: (1) extra monitoring and follow-up during class time, (2) additional instructional services during regular class time, (3) a part-time special class or resource room, (4) close to full-time placement in a classroom or resource room for direct instruction, (5) assignment to a special school or self-contained classroom within the system, or (6) placement full- or part-time outside the district. An LD student's IEP will be reviewed and revised annually. At the high school level, the student may be placed in a lower academic tract, a core curriculum or vocational work-study programs and may simultaneously receive special education services. At the elementary level, most schools will use the "pull-out" method whereby the child will go to a resource room for between 30 minutes and 2½ hours per day. Within the best resource rooms, there may be two or three students and one LD or special education teacher who goes from child to child and provides one-to-one instruction. Commonly between 2 and 5 percent of a district's population is labeled LD, and 70 percent of this group are serviced in a resource room or by an itinerant special education teacher.

When Should Parent Intervene in Child's Behalf?

It is not unusual for a parent to be unhappy with the findings of the evaluation team or to dislike features of the placements considered. A parent may feel that the gap between the child's performance in school and the expected achievement level is widening rather than diminishing under the actually implemented IEP or may find that the child has become increasingly difficult to live with. The parent must decide at this point whether it is best to stand by and hope the attitudes or behavior are part of a passing phase or whether it is best to act independently of the school. There are risks to consider at this point: (1) inaction may make matters worse, (2) overreaction may alienate those in a position to help by giving the child the upper hand in resolving conflicts between school and home and (3) premature intervention may arrest the initially slow progress being made. Every attempt should be made to resolve differences with the child's teacher and principal in an amicable fashion before beginning to shop around for alternatives. If the school is unconvinced that matters are as bad as the parent finds them and/or is unwilling to ameliorate the situation, the parent probably should intervene. Following are options worth considering.

Guidelines for Independent Action

- Notify school that second outside evaluation is desired. School must respond in writing and indicate willingness or refusal to authorize this and/or to pay for it.
- Analyze reasons for child's outbursts and reduce number of "triggers"; work out problems of sibling rivalry and resentment; find adult role models who will spend time with child; find and structure after-school social contacts so as to avoid isolation experienced by many LD students.
- Make contact with LD advocacy group such as the ACLD;

names and addresses may be obtained by calling state or national headquarters.

• Consider engaging a private tutor. An example of what may be possible is the program offered by the Developmental Learning Center in Stuart, Florida: at parent's request, tutors go into private schools and work individually with students during lunch, study hall or gym; students at a nearby public school walk to the Center during school time for the same service; students in more distant public school come in the late afternoon; tutees often move ahead two or three years in skill levels in reading readiness, reading, written expression or math in one year; parents use summer learning packets to ensure carry-over until September; the fee is $18 per hour.

• Before deciding to provide tutorial instruction oneself, consider conflicts that may arise. A child needs the parents' emotional support. Also, tutors for LD students need special training.

• Enroll child in a summer camp, either a special LD camp or a regular one. Temporary disengagements are stopgap measures, but also good therapy. The change of venue, new friends and probable maturation may be enough to restore the child's confidence and motivation.

• Contact school in writing and request a due process hearing. Parent will receive notice of date of hearing by impartial hearing officer and be informed of right to legal counsel. Purpose is to challenge school's interpretation of "appropriate." Decision will be reached within 45 days. Parent can appeal to State Department of Education for different decision. Case may be appealed later in civil court.

• Consider moving to a school district with a good reputation in the field of special education or assign legal guardianship and establish child's residence during school term with close friend or relative in this district.

• Consider enrolling child in a private or parochial school that has either desirable size and structure features or appropriate LD remediation program.

What Does Private Schooling Cost?

Cost will be an important factor in deciding the merits of placing an LD child in other than the local public school, but the parent may obtain some breaks that reduce the financial outlay. If a member of the medical profession has prescribed special schooling, the amount paid in tuition and travel may be partly deductible on one's income tax, assuming the school is remedial in nature. If the instructional emphasis is decidedly clinical, the cost may be partly reimbursable through one's insurance policy. Another way to figure the cost of alternative school placement is to ask what one might plan to spend on the child's postsecondary schooling; the investment of a comparable amount in the early years may ensure that the child gets the academic background necessary to be admitted to or to stay in a college or vocational program, the cost of which may turn out to be negligible. Currently under consideration in Congress are bills granting tuition tax credits, vouchers and other forms of remuneration to parents who send their children to private schools. Parents who pay private school tuition feel burdened by the expense, but most feel the benefits outweigh the disadvantages. Some schools award scholarships, and, of course, the state may elect to reimburse the parent and/or school for the tuition cost if it is officially determined that such placement outside of the district is most appropriate. If a family decides to bear the expense of providing alternative LD schooling, the following procedure should be helpful.

Guidelines for Finding the Most Appropriate Alternative Schooling

• Study the schools described in the *Selective Guide* section of this book, along with Chapters IV and V.
• Check out all local options by consulting the State Department of Education, advocacy groups, counselors in the educational field, parochial school headquarters and all existing guides and directories.
• Source books can be obtained through a local library or bookstore or by writing the publishing organization. These include (1) *The Directory of Facilities and Services for the Learning Disabled* (Academic Therapies), (2) *The Handbook of Private Schools* (Porter Sargent), (3) *The Directory for Exceptional Children* (Porter Sargent), (4) *The Membership Directory of the National Association of Private Schools for Exceptional Children,* (5) Peterson's *Guide to Independent Schools,* (6) The Bunting and Lyon Bluebook — *Private and Independent Schools,* (7) Lovejoy's *Prep School Guide,* (8) *Directory of Learning Resources for Learning Disabled* (Buehler, Bureau of Business Practice, Inc.) and (9) *Guide for Parents of Learning Disabled Children* (FCLD).
• From all the aforesaid sources, make list of a dozen or more likely alternatives.
• Consider residential schools. A student's almost full-time immersion in supervised school activities may be the most

efficient mode of remediation and may allow student social experiences from which he/she is excluded in peer environment of home community.

• If preference is for a regular *mainstream school* that provides supplementary remedial, developmental or corrective support on the side, the codes, symbols and charts of directories such as the Porter Sargent private school handbook, the Peterson guide, the Bluebook and the Lovejoy guide must be studied with great care. Most good prep schools do not advertise that they have remedial programs. Parochial schools that may have just the discipline and structure needed are often not listed anywhere in these guides. Nor are good public school programs usually listed.

• Write individual letters to the directors of those schools whose descriptions suggest they offer what's needed. Include a brief statement describing the child's problem and academic profile. Request school literature. Telephoning at this stage is not advised.

• Once literature has been received, select the schools that appeal most.

• Telephone school directors in order to ascertain suitability of these schools' programs to the child's need. If none seems appropriate, ask director what schools might be recommended to meet the child's particular needs.

• Narrow choices down to two or three schools. Telephone back to make arrangements to visit. Ask which records should be brought or sent and which tests will be required at school before admission and what they will cost.

• Inform the child of forthcoming travel and of choices to be made during course of joint visit. The child needs to accompany adult and vice versa on these campus visits; the input of each is important, but the child should defer to the parents' wishes. By the time each school visit is concluded, all parties concerned should sense what the verdict will be regarding acceptance, even though final word on admission may not come until evaluation of the test results is complete.

• Keep discussions of school changes calm, quiet and confidential. Although there is nothing to be ashamed of, face-saving is crucial, and excessive talk may confuse and embarrass child vis-à-vis peers and other family members.

• Before making final decisions, estimate what is involved over the course of the next five years in continuing to oversee and pay for the student's education. Most schools are able to return a student to a regular school within two or three years; some are permanent placements. Modifications of plans inevitably will occur, but, all the same, long-range planning is necessary to avoid wasteful disruptions because of unforeseen developments.

How Should Special Schooling Be Viewed?

A special school should never be considered a dumping ground, but as a therapeutic way station or haven. When the engine of a fine motor vehicle develops problems, one takes it to a professional mechanic who can remedy the situation. The child is like the motor that needs fine tuning, only he/she should be treated even more lovingly and conscientiously. It may not be easy at first to tell whether this is the kind of treatment that will be received in an individual school or classroom. Objective criteria such as the editors used in evaluating LD schools are helpful in weeding out those places that are not up to standard, but gauging the character of an institution is of necessity an intuitive, subjective determination. It is imperative that parents spend time planning a child's future; it is even more important that parents make wise and careful judgments when placing a child as vulnerable as the typical LD student. This may require several days away from work. By taking the weekday time to visit schools under consideration, parents will likely find the appropriate place for their son or daughter.

CHAPTER IV

Research Procedures Used in Compiling *A Selective Guide*

The *Selective Guide*, which comprises the major section of this book, contains descriptions of 50 exemplary LD school programs. They represent a cross section and are not a definitive compilation; many other excellent programs exist throughout the country. Of those selected, two are public, some are parochial, many are private. All are short- or long-term alternatives to the educational offerings usually found in a local public school district.

The rationale underlying the creation of the *Selective Guide* was that (1) work had to begin in finding and sorting out the types of LD schooling alternatives that were available, (2) quality programs needed and deserved to be brought to the attention of the public, and (3) a practical, systematic procedure had to be developed whereby quality could be assessed. For this guide, a multistep screening process was devised by which schools could be evaluated on the basis of their own stated goals and objectives. Common sense dictated the choice of methodology and criteria. The overriding goals of each institution governed whether criteria were applicable. Noteworthy features received particular attention and served as the keynote of each of the written reviews contained in the *Selective Guide*.

The editors knew that the establishment of a creditable methodology was of foremost importance if their guide was to serve its intended purpose. Much of the existing resource information has not been based on firsthand observation by independent evaluators, although some states and some private referral agencies maintain lists of approved educational facilities that have been visited. A few alternative schools have accrediting agencies evaluate their programs. The directories and guides mentioned in Chapter III, however, consist of data or descriptive summaries supplied mainly by the schools themselves. In some instances being listed requires the payment of a fee. No commercially available directory lists all of the alternatives that exist.

The reasons for the lack of a comprehensive LD schooling guide bear upon the problems of establishing universally accepted norms, prescribed standards and classification systems. In the field of learning disabilities, a field acknowledged publicly only 20 years ago, educational objectives are as diverse and personal as the individual students who make up a student body. Quality is elusive, abstract and subjectively determined. The only real way to judge it is through gauging quantifiable characteristics. Programs serving LD students are so irregular, though, that no good way has yet been found to quantify and compare them. Factors such as cost, size, testing scores, staff ratios, rates of academic improvement, supplementary services, postschooling achievements, space utilization, program materials and general appearance may be useful indices of how well a school is doing the job it has set for itself; but these characteristics do not fall within a consistent framework. It is understandable why no complete and authoritative LD schooling guide so far has been undertaken.

There are, even so, informal ways to make reasonable judgments about LD schools. Observation yields evidence that can be used to determine whether stated educational objectives are being met. Numerical data can be documented. Results from criterion-referenced testing enable an educator to show what students know and can do. Judgments can be made regarding the nature of the instructional climate and the physical surroundings. Explanations for obvious shortcomings can be sought; these may be taken into account and weighed against observable strengths. During a lengthy visit to a school site, qualified, experienced observers can detect whether and how program objectives are being implemented.

Several authorities in the field of special education and educational measurement helped the editors of the *Selective Guide* devise the system they used to find and evaluate the 50 schools described. A debt of gratitude is owed to Dr. Jeanette Fleischner, Ms.

Adele Handler, Dr. Robert Harth and Dr. William McLure, for their encouragement and recommendations. With their help terms were defined and criteria set forth. The particulars of the project and its execution, though, are the result of the editors' need for practicality. The parameters of this pioneer effort appeared boundless, but time and money were limited. Any plan had to be manageable.

First the current literature on schooling for the learning disabled was reviewed. Experts were consulted. Local public and private LD school facilities were visited and lay opinions were sought. Next a letter and questionnaire were prepared. Existing LD placement directories were culled in order to obtain the names and addresses of those facilities whose instructional programs served LD students between the ages of 5 and 18. The program directors of these school programs received in February of 1983 an explanatory letter; they were asked to complete and return an enclosed questionnaire by March 15. A separate mailing was sent to chairpersons of state LD advocacy groups requesting that these same enclosures be forwarded to directors of noteworthy public school programs within their states.

Responses to the first mailing were encouraging. More than 160 were returned — a remarkable rate of about 45 percent. Using predetermined criteria, the editors chose from among the responses about 100 programs for closer scrutiny. The diversity of the data obtained was astounding; there seemed to be few observable patterns.

Several factors made the selection process arduous, among them the interpretation of the meaning of the different terminology used by the directors in responding to the questionnaire. School officials naturally tend to project as positive an image as they can when describing their programs. Also, charlatans capitalize on people in desperation and will make fraudulent claims regarding the merits of their remedies. Some financially hard-pressed schools might be prone to take any paying applicants; others might be reluctant to disclose the circumstances causing staff dissension and unsatisfactory pupil progress. The editors were interested in finding and recommending programs that convincingly demonstrated that they were accomplishing what they claimed to be trying to do. The editors felt the public at large could decide if the schools' goals and objectives were compatible with the philosophy they espoused. They could also judge the appropriateness of the means used to implement a given philosophy. What the public could not assess was whether the schools were earnestly and actually pursuing their professed aims. This determination was the responsibility of those evaluating the programs.

The questionnaire was designed to pinpoint programs for LD children of normal or above average intelligence and to eliminate those serving the mentally retarded and/or the severely emotionally disturbed. Respondents were asked to indicate if they offered sports, fine arts, motor and visual training, sensory integration, diagnostic testing, vocational programs and counseling services. Low teacher/pupil ratios and small class sizes were deemed a crucial asset.

Four geographic areas were mapped out: the Northeast, the Southeast, the Midwest and the Far West. Within each area a representative sample of schools was selected for follow-up. A balance was sought between large and small schools, day and residential ones, low-priced and expensive ones, and rural and urban settings. Additional checking took place with educational contacts in the vicinity of each school under consideration. The directors of the selected programs were then telephoned in order to schedule appointments to visit. Not all schools among those that replied were accessible, given the editors' self-imposed timetable, their budget and the logistics involved. Arranging a visitation time was occasionally impossible because of the timing of the spring or summer breaks at certain schools. In order that the maximum number of schools might be visited, six qualified persons were enlisted and trained.

Members of the evaluation team followed a uniform set of instructions. Investigative and interview techniques were perfected. They used a four-page checklist that covered the areas of (1) physical plant and facilities, (2) staff, (3) curriculum and (4) testing and evaluative procedures. This checklist served as a guideline by which to assess and rank 64 different aspects of the school program. Ways of determining the strength of these attributes were prescribed.

During each school visit, the evaluators sought to find out if the student body included the mentally retarded and/or severely disturbed students along with the LD. Within each classroom visited, the evaluators observed the nature of student time on task, the individualization and grouping practices as well as the kind of organization, structure, management and content the teachers provided. In the residential schools the investigators looked for aesthetically appealing and psychologically wholesome living situations. The special interest and physical education programs were appraised, and the presence of computers and computer training programs was noted. The critical areas of reading and language instruction were studied by classroom observation and scanning student folders and texts. The ways in which multisensory instructional approaches were incorporated into the program, the caliber and morale of the staff, the kind and amount of in-service and free teacher time all were taken into account.

Besides needing to know from the program directors what were the distinctive and successful features of their educational programs, the evaluators and editors wanted to know how and whether they might confirm their data findings. The more willing directors were to supply sources for substantiation, the more comfortable the evaluators were in trusting their first-hand observations. No school is included in the *Selective Guide* which was not in the evaluator's opinion honest, open and cooperative. Schools are frequently reluctant to allow outsiders to observe classes or to query students, teachers or parents, since this practice often is disruptive and an invasion of privacy. In this situation, however, denial of this opportunity jeopardized the evaluation. All schools in the guide permitted full access to students and staff. The visits included an inspection of the grounds, the dormitory rooms where applicable, the nonconfidential files, the dining facilities, the faculty lounges and the lavatories.

The investigators tried to ascertain the financial condition of each school visited, since undue dependence on the vagaries of reimbursements for state-funded students or on tuition increases was felt to be detrimental to conscientious program planning and implementation. Schools with rapid or frequent turnover of administration and staff required extra sleuthing. An important basis for assessing the nature and quality of a school was the appearance and conduct of students in relatively unsupervised situations, such as lunchtime or recess. Usually the evaluator ate lunch with students. The method of progress reporting to parents was considered significant. When regular parent conferences were impractical because of distance or other factors, supplementary narrative reports were deemed necessary, especially when letter grades were given on report cards. Among the many facets of the school program given consideration, perhaps the most decisive component was the degree of success and improvement that students experienced in academic masteries and feelings of self-worth. For this, the evaluators relied on their faith in the truthfulness of the director and the staff, as well as their own overall impressions of student attitudes.

The director of research and her team visited more schools than are included in the *Selective Guide.* Those not included may have been undergoing major organizational changes; they may have been the object of widespread local controversy; they may have been unable during the time allowed to satisfy the evaluators as to the essentials of their program. The goals and objectives of a given program might have been too fuzzy. Some schools rated poorly overall. In some cases the learning environments of schools visited were too unpleasant or disruptive to receive the evaluator's endorsement.

Each evaluator supplied the editors with a written review of the program observed. After editing, these reviews have been published without the schools' having been provided an opportunity to see or change the contents. This policy of not allowing the schools to correct or approve what was written about them carries with it the possibility that inadvertent errors may be present. However, since all school programs included were ones that favorably impressed the evaluators, it was felt the schools would not be offended by anything mentioned.

Readers should note that the information contained in each review is based on the situation found to exist between the spring and September of 1983. Specific data regarding enrollment figures, costs, program offerings and the like are subject to change. Because staff changes regularly occur within schools, the names of school personnel are given in only a few instances.

The programs described in the *Selective Guide* represent a broad cross section of LD placement alternatives ranging from the very specialized schools serving only dyslexic children, for example, to private prep schools that have adapted their programs to accommodate limited numbers of LD students. Several schools work with the child of below average intelligence, and one school is geared especially to the gifted college-bound young man. Some schools serve severely handicapped LD youngsters with concomitant emotional problems; others serve only those with mildly to moderately severe disabilities.

The editors were and are pleased to find such a wide variety of good alternatives available to the LD child. The findings and impressions of the evaluation team members were such that they are eager to continue the work begun and to broaden and delineate further the scope of the study. One team member, a veteran educator and investigative reporter, decided he wanted to go back to being a teacher, so impressed was he by what he observed. He felt that if the enthusiasm, dedication and professionalism that he witnessed could be incorporated into every classroom of America the crisis in education could be solved. Another evaluator felt the answer to the educational dilemmas of the 80s was to make all education special, to give every student an individual educational program, to zero in on the unique learning styles of human beings and to adapt classroom instructional strategies accordingly. Each investigator completed his or her assignment with a greater appreciation for the work being done in the LD field. All felt that schools included in the guide were ones to which they would send their own child, should the child require placement outside of a local school.

CHAPTER V

Patterns and Findings From the Study

Native to human beings is the ability to infer or deduce. Inevitably the authors of the *Selective Guide* drew general conclusions from their six months' study of schooling for the learning disabled. These generalizations are debatable and subject to criticism. They are tentative, for as yet documentation is insufficient. They are shared with readers in the hope that these impressions may be subsequently tested for validity and reliability. Professionals in the educational field may find the observations that follow quite obvious and common-sensical. Others may find them not nearly so apparent.

One glaring discovery was that many school brochures are deceptive. Even when the authors carefully scrutinized the small print of public relations materials prior to visiting, they were sometimes startled by what they found on arrival.

Although it was expected that where tuition was covered by families, students at special LD schools would be from upper middle class backgrounds, the authors were surprised by the sacrifices made by many from lower social-economic levels. The assumption had been that the financial status, educational background and social standing of parents were major determinants of the willingness to finance alternative schooling. What seemed more important, though, was the intensity of parental concern.

Several criteria that initially were thought to be good indicators of school quality proved to be nonpredictive. The per-pupil cost did not correlate with quality. Neither did the spaciousness and aesthetic appeal of the facility. The extent of parental involvement with the school program did not seem to matter.

The good school programs all had able, efficient and energetic directors. Another key factor seemed to be the staff: their competence, their dedication, their rapport with the school administration and the number of students for whom they were personally responsible. Prior teaching experience was a decided plus, and experience within a regular classroom was particularly valuable. The tendency among such former "regular" teachers was to view their students as normal, albeit different; this outlook affected the way expectations were expressed, consciously or subconsciously. Less mollycoddling tended to occur. Certification in special education or learning disabilities affected the proficiency with which special learning deficits were addressed in most instances. Also, the more experienced the staff, the more eclectic the approach and the more prescriptive the teaching. But on-the-job training yielded almost comparable results. Special knowledge or advanced training in the underlying structure of a particular discipline seemed particularly meritorious in the transmission of essential understanding in the areas of language and math. Schools where teachers had little free or flexible time in their schedules yielded proportionately greater frenzy and more teacher burnout.

Schools where teachers were not carefully supervised and/or where the progress of individual students was not carefully monitored were ones with fuzzy overall program objectives. Simultaneously, schools where teachers felt they had a stake in the program, where the plan was not arbitrarily superimposed but jointly determined in a team way, seemed most successful.

Accordingly, the smaller the school, the better the communication between professional staff members and the more expeditious the remediation of student deficiencies. When staff members were close and cohesive, they could concentrate their collective energies and talents on the reinforcement of positive behaviors. This also facilitated speedy, frequent communication between home and school. Residential schools tended to minimize the value of intense home-school communication. This may be explained by the need and intent of boarding schools to develop student self-reliance and also to keep their students fully occupied.

The smaller the class, the better. In classes of 12 or more where the teacher lectured, children's minds tended to wander, hands and feet tended to explore and in some cases classes were out of control. Time was wasted. The larger classes that had an aide allowed the teachers to give individual help as needed and seemed to work better, for the children stayed more focused on their tasks. Exceptions were the transition classes that approximated a regular classroom situation.

A correlation seemed to exist between the selectivity of the school's admissions and the speed with which remediation occurred. The less focused the program, the longer the student stayed. On the other hand, in those situations where the school emphasis was on attitudinal change, the length of stay was not really relevant. Transitional classes were considered valuable to later school adjustment. Transitional programs were usually accompanied by intense efforts to place children appropriately after leaving the school.

It was found true that the earlier the diagnosis and subsequent remediation, the better the child's prognosis and his subsequent social and academic adjustment. An LD child knows he is "different" but doesn't know why. The early remediation alleviated the frustration and heartbreak usually associated with an LD handicap.

Federal law provides special preschool training at public expense to those eligible. Examples of good programs available in some states are the public school programs in Baltimore County, Maryland, for children 18 months and older; the program at the private Speech and Language Center of Northern Virginia for two-year-olds; the public preschools in Ohio modeled on the individualized programs instituted in Catawba and Springfield, Ohio; and the state funded mainstreaming of handicapped preschoolers at the Stepping Stones Nursery School in Minnesota for either 2½ or 11 hours per day.

Tutoring by those trained in the special methods used to teach LD children was shown to be helpful. Conversely, tutors not trained in these specific techniques tended to reinforce learning patterns that hadn't worked previously and to increase the frustration of both tutor and pupil. This perhaps explains why the better schools discouraged parents from helping their children with homework. Day schools tended to use homework for reinforcement; boarding facilities, which often required two or more hours of daily after-school work usually provided trained teachers to solve problems immediately. The cost of private tutoring was found to range from between $18 to $35 per hour.

Many day school students spent up to two hours commuting. The authors felt that proximity to school was neither a detriment nor an asset to the educational benefit received.

As former teachers, the evaluation team was astounded by the professionalism and dedication of the teachers they encountered and by the fact that so many private school teachers worked so hard for so little money. These teachers, who earned in some instances less than half the salary of those in the public sector, spent a larger proportion of their time at school. In residential schools, they were expected to attend evening meetings, meet with parent groups, supervise recreational activities and spend weekends on campus to confer with parents or oversee students. Teachers in the day schools often led informational meetings for parents in the evenings, took their charges on weekend outings, wrote extensive reports to parents and very seldom left at the 3 o'clock bell.

Another finding was that boys substantially outnumbered girls in these special schools. Reasons for this vary, but many experts now believe that girls may not have been properly diagnosed in the past and that educators will be seeing more and more girls labeled LD.

Messiness and disorganization in dorms or classrooms seemed counterproductive to the goals of the schools, almost all of which stated they tried to foster order and structure in youngsters' lives.

Interesting geographical differences surfaced as the researchers visited throughout the country. In California, for instance, prior to Proposition 13 and P.L. 94-142, school districts funded many LD students at private boarding facilities outside the state since virtually no boarding facilities existed in California. This has all but ceased. New criteria established by California in 1983 mandate that children be labeled SH (severely handicapped) to be eligible for publicly funded services at special educational facilities within the state. Severely handicapped youngsters include the learning handicapped (LH), physically handicapped (PH), emotionally handicapped (EH) and communicatively handicapped (CH). (Subsumed within the LD category are the educable mentally retarded (EMR), the behaviorally disordered (BD) and the learning disabled. If a learning disabled child's problem is severe, he may be in a classroom with psychotic or autistic children.) Placement is determined by the *severity* of the specific disability. Thus, the LD child, before being eligible for many special public school services may wait until he is 2.5 standard deviations below the mean (4 years). Students who are mildly learning disabled and non-funded in California are flocking to private schools that cropped up all over the state between 1977 and 1980.

The East Coast, on the other hand, has long had a tradition of private special and preparatory schools. Parents are used to paying so that their children might attend such schools. Californians have expected their school districts to "pick up the tab." So, along the Eastern Seaboard, LD schools, day and boarding, not only are more established, they are often quite selective in their admissions. The good ones tend to be homogeneous. The mildly LD attend one kind of school, the more severely LD attend with others like themselves; the emotionally disturbed are in another school. Because many private California schools accept state-funded students whose disability is severe, classrooms there are very heterogeneous.

A lack of good, private special educational facilities in the Midwest is obvious if one looks at this book's small section for this locale. In suburban and metropolitan areas, the public school programs tend to be adequate. The outlying areas around Chicago, once known as the fertile crescent of LD, offer particularly diverse and satisfactory services. Rural areas throughout the Midwest tended to be unaware of learning disabilities or at least to provide minimal screening and prescriptive teaching.

The authors hope these initial general findings may be incorporated into a more sophisticated statistical analysis based on more school observations and comparative data.

CHAPTER VI

An Invitation

In concluding this section of *Schooling for the Learning Disabled*, the editors wish to issue an invitation. *The Selective Guide to LD Programs in Elementary and Secondary Schools Throughout the United States* contains descriptions of 50 diverse programs. A need exists to explore more of the alternatives available. Therefore, the directors of LD schools and programs in both the private and public sector are invited to indicate their interest in receiving an evaluation visit during the upcoming year. An enlarged and updated edition of *Schooling for the Learning Disabled* is anticipated in 1984/1985, and the editors welcome any suggestions that will aid them in extending the scope, usefulness and purpose of their initial compilation. Inquiries and suggestions may be addressed to the SMS Publishing Corporation, P.O. Box 2276, Glenview, IL, 60025.

A Selective Guide

to LD Programs in
Elementary and Secondary Schools
Throughout the United States

eeeeeeeeeeeeeeeeeeeeeeeeeeeeeeeeeeeeeeeeeeeeeeeeeeeeeeeeeeee

SCHOOLS OF THE NORTHEAST

CHURCHILL SCHOOL
22 E. 95th St.
New York, NY 10028

Private/Coed
Day
Enrollment 82
Ages 5-13

Churchill is a school on the move. Innovation has high priority and is a forerunner of educational excellence. Both innovation and excellence are found in abundance in this little "bursting-at-the-seams" school which is located in a once-elegant, old greystone mansion, a few steps from New York City's Central Park.

A visitor's attention is immediately drawn to the large and friendly staff. Eight teachers, all having earned Master's degrees in special education, are available to teach the 82 elementary school-aged children. In addition to the teaching staff, the school employs two LD specialists who test and evaluate the progress of each student and work with the teachers in an advisory capacity. Other support staff include two qualified language therapists for those children exhibiting communication problems, an occupational therapist and a school psychologist. That the staff love their work is obvious; they enthusiastically explain the detailed workings of their program and invite the visitor to view their sessions with the children.

Openness characterizes Churchill. The staff, like the children, are young, enthusiastic and fun-loving. A buzz of activity fills the three floors of the building. Children are everywhere—coming and going to gym classes and outings, studying art in the park or the corridors, and even having an extra tutoring session on the stairs. Space is dear at the school, but structure is evident. The children are unaware of any underlying control, for it does not interfere with the excitement and satisfaction of learning.

Students are grouped in small, non-graded, self-contained classes of eight to ten children. Each student's core curriculum includes reading, handwriting, spelling, mathematics and social science and is individualized for each child. Language is taught by integrating reading, spelling and writing around central themes. Phonics and conceptual analysis of reading material are stressed, and an extensive variety of materials and approaches is used to carry out each child's individual program.

No gymnasium is located in the building, but all students receive 45 minutes of physical education daily. Classes are held in Central Park and at the 92nd Street "Y." Art classes are held within the self-contained classrooms. Computers are budgeted for 1984. Available within walking distance of the school are some of New York's finest museums and cultural attractions which Churchill uses to extend instruction beyond the classroom walls.

A real hit with both staff and students is "Project Heroes," an innovative social studies program designed by the staff and now in use at Churchill and classrooms around the country. Its content-oriented curriculum, developed to excite the imagination and curiosity of the LD child, is built around the study of famous "heroes" like Thomas Edison and Hans Christian Andersen who succeeded in life despite learning difficulties. "Biographical study begins with the child's own world, moves to the life of a hero, and expands to the broader world in which the hero lived." The children gather facts about the historical and cultural backgrounds of each hero in museums and libraries and then explore the art, literature, architecture, and political climate of his times. Churchill's children relate to these heroes who too were once labeled as "slow learners," "lazy," or "daydreamers" by their parents and teachers. The important lesson learned is that the specific label of LD can become irrelevant and that life was not always smooth and easy for these individuals.

Parents wishing to place their child at Churchill School meet with the admissions director for an initial interview and a tour of the school. After the school receives the prior educational and psychological evaluations and if the child seems to be an appropriate candidate, he or she is interviewed by the school psychologist. The admissions committee then decides regarding placement. Churchill admits only those children with average or above average intelligence manifesting a specific learning disability. Upon admission, each child receives a complete learning disabilities evaluation by the staff. Areas tested include receptive and expressive language, visual and auditory perception, visual motor integration, and conceptual and abstract abilities. Skills tests for academics are also administered.

Remediation begins once a learning profile is obtained. The program is based upon utilization of strengths to remediate deficits through an individual education plan. Each child receives on-going diagnosis through weekly teacher meetings, periodic retesting and reassessment.

Parents play an important, active role at Churchill through membership in the Parents' Association, in committee work, at staff-designed workshops and at monthly parent meetings. The association's goal is "to promote cooperation and communication between parents and school and to encourage parent involvement in Churchill."

Churchill's goal is to return the child to the regular classroom. A placement director works closely with the child and his parents to find the most suitable future school. According to her, 50 percent of Churchill students are mainstreamed after three years, and another 25 percent eventually take their place there. Tuition cost is $7,800; a limited number of scholarships are available for the 40 percent of Churchill's students not funded by local school districts.

Not content with just being an excellent school, Churchill is committed to sharing its knowledge and expertise with the community at large. In 1980, the Churchill Center for Learning Disabilities was established and has since sponsored, in conjunction with The Buckley School, New York University, The Bank Street School of Education and Teachers College/Columbia University, an outreach program consisting of workshops, courses, seminars and conferences, which helps to extend Churchill's work in learning disabilities "beyond the school to parents and the educational community at large." The Center also publishes *The Churchill Forum*, a quarterly newspaper focusing on issues in the LD field. Despite the rather crowded conditions and the lack of such amenities as art rooms and gymnasiums, Churchill has many strengths: a sensitive, hard-working, creative staff; a warm, friendly and open atmosphere; and an excellent curriculum. Most children are happy and productive and seem not to miss these "extras;" they think Churchill is a "great school."

THE COMMUNITY SCHOOLS
OF BERGEN COUNTY

The two separate campuses, staffs and age-grouped student bodies of the private, ungraded Community School represent a distinctive and effective answer to the question of how to educate severely LD children. One campus for boys and girls of from kindergarten through junior high age is located on a 3½-acre estate in a pleasant, residential area of Bergen County, New Jersey, across the Hudson River from Manhattan. The high school, 15 miles away, occupies a former elementary school. Tuition for both schools is $6,800.

THE COMMUNITY SCHOOL
(Elementary and Junior High School)
420 Booth Ave.
Englewood, NJ 07631.

Private/Coed
Day
Enrollment 86
Ages 5-14

Here, very small classes allow close individual attention to be lavished upon the 86 children who attend. The staff consists of twenty-six teachers, an adaptive physical education instructor, an occupational therapist, a speech and language specialist, two psychologists, two remedial reading specialists, a library resource teacher, and three para-professionals. These youngsters, many of whom have serious academic, social and behavioral problems, are well-provided with the help they need to develop their capabilities. Community School children are of low average to superior intelligence; their potential exceeds their past performance and they work best when in a personal, caring environment. Their problems are varied: some fit the classic LD profile; some have autistic tendencies, some evince schizophrenic behavior and others are slow learners. The teachers and support staff work so closely with each student they can usually diffuse potentially explosive situations.

"Crisis intervention" is on hand, but is very seldom used. Classes are exceptionally well-managed. The school's experienced, highly qualified teachers know how to keep youngsters too busy for troublemaking. Two thirds of the students receive funding at this fine, reasonably priced school. The main school building is in a converted mansion which holds administrative offices and middle school classrooms (grades 4 - 6). Two annexes house the lower (Kdg. - 3) and upper school (7 - 9).

The ability-grouped classes have an average of four students. The middle and upper school homeroom groups remain together for English, language, social studies, spelling and writing. Classes are departmentalized in reading, mathematics, science, shop, art, computers, physical education, health, and individual tutoring. Reading classes use a prescriptive approach; the method is determined by need as set forth in each student's IEP. An occupational therapist works with the lower school. Each day, a different modality is emphasized: (1) gross motor, (2) fine motor, (3) language arts, (4) sensory integration and (5) music.

Students are busy with more than reading, writing and arithmetic. They build bird feeders and bookshelves in the woodshop; paint, draw, sculpt and pot in art class; operate the five computers; and take off on field trips to cultural attractions nearby.

Daily physical education is offered outside; there is no gymnasium. Team sports in football, soccer, softball, volleyball and street hockey are played. The major event of the year is the school olympics where students vie for medals and certificates. An extra class in movement is designed for those students needing gross motor control work. Individual adaptive physical education is offered for select students.

The school's behavior management program is a highly visible and, according to the teachers, successful method of dealing with such negative behaviors as physical aggression, verbal aggression, inappropriate language, spitting, throwing objects, and refusal to do required classwork. All classes have a color wheel in the room. Red, yellow, and green denote specific behaviors allowed at that time. Students are given both behavior and effort points to be used for special "perks" such as monthly workshops or ski trips. Infractions result in removal to the *Time Out Room,* to in-school suspensions or parent conferences.

Since Community opened in 1968, parents have been encouraged to become and stay involved with the school. Evening programs on learning disabilities, behavior management and other related topics are held each month. Parents are invited to take an active part in the development of their child's IEP. An active parents' association raises funds for buying school "extras", such as a new computer.

Community does a good job with its diverse student body. It believes each child is eager to achieve; and the staff's psychodynamic approach manages to activate this inner drive.

COMMUNITY HIGH SCHOOL
15 Columbus Rd.
Demarest, NJ 07627

Private/Coed
Day
Enrollment 82
Ages 14-21

The program at Community High is a pragmatic one that combines academic fundamentals and vocational training for its 82 students. This works well for the high school's diverse student body, for, upon graduation, 50 percent attend two and four year college programs, 25 percent attend vocational schools and the remaining 25 percent move directly into the work force.

The vocational program includes a guidance course which explores different career options and familiarizes students with the skills needed to acquire and hold a job. In the industrial arts facet of the program, students learn specific skills in the areas of small engine repair, woodworking, electrical and plumbing maintenance, typing and graphic arts. Home economics covers cooking and nutrition. Five computer courses, which teach processing and programming, are offered in the computer room with its bank of ten terminals.

The academic program is based on a standard high school curriculum. The ability-grouped classes may have as few as one or as many as eight students. An experienced, credentialed staff follows a discussion format. Students respond eagerly, but in a controlled and well-behaved way.

A daily study skills class is provided for the bright, college-bound student who has serious organizational problems. Strategies for studying, following directions, organizing time and taking SAT tests are stressed.

A post-graduate program is available to those who are enrolled part-time in college but who need extra reinforcement. The usual pattern is for students to take two courses at a local community college along with two additional college level courses and counseling at Community.

The teaching staff numbers 26. In addition, an LD specialist, a speech and language therapist, two physical education teachers and two remedial reading teachers see youngsters on a one-on-one basis or in small groups.

Extra-curricular activities include student council, intramural activities, theatre, photography, ski trips, ceramics, chorus, graphics, drama club, and planned trips to local and NYC theatres. A school newspaper is published three times a year, and a yearbook is produced by the students.

Good interpersonal relationships and coping skills are stressed in weekly group counseling sessions. Individual counseling can be arranged, when needed, with the psychological staff that serve both schools.

Parents are encouraged to attend the special evening programs given at the lower school. Numerical grades are sent home four times per year, and written narratives are sent three times. As 80 percent of Community's students are funded by their school districts, an annual IEP review is held which parents are expected to attend.

Community High is a basic day school program tailored to fit a wide variety of students and needs. The ability range of Community's students is from low average to superior (85 to 140 IQ). The boys and girls don't fit the prep school image; there's no dress code here. But, the teenagers are well-behaved and friendly; they like their school. In fact, many of them come back each year for alumni day to share remembrances and swap stories of present successes.

EAGLE HILL SCHOOL
45 Glenville Rd.
Greenwich, CT 06830

Coed
Private/Boys
Day/Residential
Enrollment 135
Ages 6-16

Parents from wealthy communities north of New York City whose children had attended Eagle Hill of Massachusetts wanted something similar closer to home. In 1975, their desires were satisfied with the establishment of a second Eagle Hill. Located in the gently rolling hills of Greenwich, Connecticut, on a 20-acre tract of land formerly owned by Marjorie Merriweather Post, the campus consists of a handsome, old, fieldstone gatehouse, a mansion and sundry nearby buildings. The students, 105 boys and 30 girls between the ages of 6 and 16, come primarily from the counties of Westchester, New York and Fairfield, Connecticut. A majority are day students, attending classes from 8:30 AM to 4:15 PM; only 30 boys and 8 girls reside on campus. Tuition is $11,200 for the day students and $16,200 for the boarders. About $80,000 to $85,000 in partial scholarship money is granted each year, a rather impressive amount for a school as small and as new as Eagle Hill. A very active parent association, which functions as a separate corporation, raises much of this money.

Eagle Hill's philosophy is to give its students the skills needed to deal with a complex society. So, along with special math and language arts instruction, the school partially integrates its students with those in regular educational settings. Both boys and girls participate in a big interscholastic sports program, which includes cross country skiing, soccer, baseball, ice-hockey, basketball and tennis. They are the only special school members of the Fairchester (Fairfield and Westchester counties) League. The students also attend cultural events and go on field trips with the League schools.

Eagle Hill has an outdoor playing field and tennis court; otherwise physical education classes are held at a facility in Greenwich. Library resources in town are also used, as the school has no student library. Planned for 1984 is a center for a gymnasium, science labs and art rooms.

Extracurricular activities, everything from art to zoology, abound at Eagle Hill. Teachers constantly share their special hobby interests with students. One teacher, an electric model train buff, set up his extensive equipment at the school, enabling everyone to discover first-hand the fun of model railroading.

The educational program at Eagle Hill stresses linguistics and total language development. Each student receives tutorial instruction once or twice daily as his needs dictate. He may progress gradually from one-on-one tutorials to groups containing three other pupils. The ungraded classes contain an average of eight age- and skill-matched students who are taught on a tightly structured group basis in major content areas.

Teachers expect and receive attentive and controlled behavior. The school's objective is to see that the child succeeds. "Nowhere is he faced with a learning situation that will make impossible demands on him". Classroom learning frustrations are negligible.

The staff includes 38 full-time teachers, three supervisors, an educational director, a school psychologist, two speech therapists and a motor skills teacher who works with those few students needing help in gross motor skills development. Primarily young and female, most of the teachers are certified in special education. On-campus training is required of new instructors. Many of the staff and their families live on campus, and several live in the dormitory.

Dorm rooms in the old fieldstone mansion accommodate two youngsters and afford each ample space. Meals are served in a spacious, first-floor dining room. Kids congregate in an adjacent lounging area before and after supervised evening study.

Admission procedures include a parental interview, usually conducted after Eagle Hill has received diagnostic information concerning the child. A diagnostic clinic, located on the grounds, operates as a separate facility under the auspices of the Eagle Hill Foundation. If necessary, the clinic will do a prospective student evaluation, but there is a rather lengthy waiting list for testing appointments. Following the parent interview, the child spends two days on campus. He makes the rounds of classes and learns that he must abide by the dress code: no jeans, T-shirts or sneakers. If he survives this shock and still wants to attend, he is evaluated by the teachers and a determination is made regarding acceptance and group placement.

Eagle Hill seeks to make academic success its own reward and has structured an environment to ensure its students a successful adaptation to the future. Its financial status promises the continuation of this excellent program.

EAGLE HILL SCHOOL
Old Petersham Rd.
Hardwick, MA 01037

Private/Boys
Residential
Enrollment 80
Ages 8-18

Bring a camera to Eagle Hill. This school is reached by passing through Hardwick, Massachusetts, a sparkling New England town of white clapboard buildings that stands sentinel-like around a center green. Eagle Hill, down the road a few miles, looks like an extension of exquisite

Hardwick. Its main building, a gracious colonial homestead built in 1759, dominates the 150-acre campus.

The school was founded in 1967, specifically to educate learning disabled boys. A warm intimacy envelopes the place, which won't change, according to the headmaster; there are no plans to increase the size beyond 90. At present, 80 boys, aged 8 to 18, from widely diverse backgrounds, attend. A rather international flavor exists with students from 28 states, Mexico, Canada, Central America and Europe in residence. Tuition is $8,945 per school year; the fee for boarding is $5,960.

Eagle Hill can meet the needs of a wide range of learning disabled children, but great care is taken to accept only those who score 90 or above on the WISC-R and can fit into an existing group and thus into the overall program. To this end, a child comes to the school with a wealth of diagnostic testing. Upon acceptance, he is assigned both an educational and a residential case manager. The educational case manager handles approximately 25 students and is responsible for developing their individual educational plans. Teachers keep track of any problems by means of a daily log for each child in their class. This information is reviewed daily by the case manager, and if needed, appropriate academic help will be given or a session will be arranged with one of the residential counselors. The cooperative, systematic coordination between the residential and educational staff is an impressive aspect of Eagle Hill.

Because success builds self-esteem, success is the major tenet of the Eagle Hill philosophy. Teachers must make sure the child succeeds in class. Accordingly, the program is so coordinated among all teachers that the student is never presented with material in any class that is beyond his instructional level. Boys at Eagle Hill cannot avoid success. The children are grouped according to their skills in classes that may contain one to eight students. A daily tutorial is an intregal part of the program; these intensive language therapy sessions deal with specific needs.

Another goal of Eagle Hill is to return the child to a regular school setting within two years, but the school does give an approved high school diploma. There are GED classes to prepare those boys 17 years and older to take the high school equivalency examination.

The entire curriculum is oriented to the basics and skill building and does not offer many optional courses except Spanish, typing, computer programming, photography and woodshop. All children must take a writing workshop. The school's small library has enough resource material for the research papers required.

Sixty percent of the young staff live on campus. The teachers are primarily female, but an all-male residential staff handles the evening supervised study halls as well as the extensive afternoon and evening hobby and sports programs. Four counselors serve in a special "listening" capacity, both for those boys who might feel the need to talk and for those whose teachers feel they need to be "talked to" or counseled.

The dormitories are attractive and functional. Most rooms house two boys and are big enough for each one to have his own desk, work space and stereo. Everybody has stereos, all playing at once. Evening study halls are held in dorm rooms with residential staff members on watch. One hour of study hall is followed by one-half hour of "quiet time" in which the boy is free to do anything he wants so long as he is quiet about it. Afterwards, the boys might play a game of pool in the recreation hall or a little basketball over at the gym before an early lights out.

Eagle Hill offers a full sports program and many extracurricular activities. In addition to its many intramural sports, the school fields interscholastic teams in cross country, soccer, basketball, skiing, volleyball, baseball, tennis and softball. A fully equipped gymnasium is the center for sports and recreational activities, and the school's very own ski hill affords hours of fun. A small island near Bar Harbor, Maine, was recently purchased by the school for use in its outward-bound program. "Students camp out for long weekends there in the autumn and spring."

The boys don't lack for something to do in their spare time at Eagle Hill. Many utilize the well-stocked arts and crafts building, the photography lab and woodworking shop. In fact, extra-curricular activities are too many to list. The school has everything from archery and bocce ball to swamp study and stained glass making. When the sap is running, it's syrup makin' time, and the boys tap enough to sell and to use in the dining room.

Eagle Hill wants its students to function independently and responsibly. To accomplish this goal, the rules are relaxed as boys show they can handle freedom. They can set their own hours, skip breakfast, study when and where they want, and in other ways escape supervision.

In attesting to the quality of the school, one 16-year-old student said: "Eagle Hill turned my whole life around. I came here with a first grade reading level two years ago, and I am now at a 9th grade reading level. I am doing extremely well, and I am very proud of myself." Personal accounts like this one are what Eagle Hill is all about.

THE FORMAN SCHOOL
Norfolk, Rd.
Litchfield, CT 06759

Private/Coed
Residential/Day
Enrollment 216
Ages 13-20

The senior high school boy or girl who meets the exacting Forman admissions criteria and is accepted at Forman School has a great time. The coeducational Forman experience is educationally sound and fun.

The school admits two types of students: those of average to bright ability exhibiting developmental dyslexia or, as Forman terms it, "learning differences," and those who have fallen behind and need a structured environment in order to "keep up" with a normal high school academic program. About 20 percent of the student body is in this latter category. According to headmaster Richard Pierce, Foreman's version of mainstreaming is advantageous to both the LD and the regular student.

This private boarding school is crowded, so much so that several students live off campus in private homes. Forman had to turn away 165 qualified applicants in 1983. The school currently has 216 students, 201 boarding and 15 day. Tuition is $9,000 for boarders and $5,000 for just the day program. Only two students are funded. Incidental expenses come to about $1,000 for the year. An extra fee of $2,600 is charged for the optional one-to-one daily language training (LT) program, which is based on an Orton-Gillingham phonics approach and is the core of Forman's program. About 70 percent of the students are enrolled. A daily one-on-one mathematics training (MT) is provided for the same fee. With extra courses, tuition at Forman can come to $14,200. While daily LT is recommended for the dyslexic student, some combine LT and MT by taking three days of language training and two of math.

Aside from the individual one-to-one instruction, Forman follows a college preparatory curriculum comparable to that of a regular high school. Most students remain the entire four years and graduate by earning credits in English (4); history (3); science (2); and six electives. Ninth graders must take a study skills course, and tenth graders are encouraged to attend a course in human sexuality. Classes are grouped according to grade level; freshman are with other freshmen, seniors with other seniors. However, certain classes such as calculus and advanced English and science, are geared for the brighter student. New is ESL (English as a Second Language) for foreign students who come from five continents. School is in session five and a half days per week. There are two schedules, one for the spring and fall, and another for the winter to accommodate skiing. Winter classes begin at 7:45 AM and last until 1:30 PM, after which the ski busses go out. Spring and fall classes go from 8:15 AM until 2:45 PM and are followed by athletics until 5 PM.

Recently built Williams Hall, one of the three academic buildings on campus, has particularly spacious classrooms and three large ultramodern laboratories. All classrooms are like the school itself, clean and neat. The school library in Carpenter Hall contains study carrels and 6,000 volumes.

A big plus, from the students' viewpoint, is the school's walking distance from town. They're not often in town, for there's so much to do on campus, but, as quipped, "It's there!". The town of Litchfield, Connecticut, with its white colonial mansions, expansive green lawns, small shops, restaurants and town square is the quintessential New England town. Seniors and Green Key members are allowed time in town on their own for a change of pace.

The school is beautifully laid out like a small village on 140 acres of woodlands, fields and ponds. The dormitories surround a common and in the center stands a huge, leafy maple, under which the yearly commencement takes place. Most of the dormitories (eight boys', three girls') are gracious homesteads, some built during the colonial and revolutionary eras. Beecher House, a boy's dorm, was the birthplace of Harriet Beecher Stowe. The bedrooms in these well-kept antique buildings are for either two, three or four. Although often small, all students have desks, storage space and at least half a closet. The common rooms in each dorm all have TV and usually a fireplace. The seldom-deserted dorms are used during study breaks and as student activity centers. Students study in their dorms at night, unless they and their homework didn't pass muster in class, in which case they have a two-hour supervised study hall. All dorms are monitored by live-in faculty members. Boys are not allowed in girls' dorms and vice-versa without permission of the house parent. Nevertheless, the campus atmosphere is open and relaxed. Students are expected to act as mature and responsible individuals.

Students who garner six demerits for rules infractions are confined to campus for two weekends. Those few who manage to accumulate 12 demerits get to visit the "review board," made up of three students, three teachers and the faculty head of the Board.

In the evenings and on weekends, students may shed required schooltime attire — jackets and ties for boys, skirts or dress slacks for girls — put on casual clothes, relax and have fun. Year-round swimming, tennis outdoors and indoors, basketball, a workout in the weight room, special activity clubs, such as yearbook, newspaper, filmmaking, drama, chess, the campus TV show and campus dances, are some of the activities that keep hands and minds busy. Camping, fishing, skiing and cultural events in nearby Hartford draw students away on weekends. Students in good standing may take two long weekends each term, and there are unlimited short weekends from Saturday afternoon to Sunday evening. Students like to spend free hours at their "Union," snacking, smoking, playing video games or pool or football. Students plan the union activities, buy and serve the food for the snack bar and are responsible for the upkeep. Student creativity is so alive that some teens decided to buy their own full-sized, fully equipped fire engine. They became proficient fire fighters, helped the local fire department and taught cardiopulmonary resuscitation and lifesaving techniques to other students.

Athletics play an important part in the life of the Formanite. All students participate. Some compete at the varsity or junior varsity level, while others engage less competitively in soccer, cross-country, basketball, squash, skiing, swimming, baseball, tennis, lacrosse, volleyball and golf. Camping, environmental awareness, karate, dance and horseback riding are also part of the physical education program.

Fine arts are stressed almost as much as sports at Forman. The school has an excellent program under the direction of its long-term teacher Richard Doyle. LIGHT GREEN PRODUCTIONS (a mixture of the school colors of white and green) perform three plays a year: one classical, one original, and a dinner theatre production in which both faculty and students take part and which is *the* event of the year. LIGHT GREEN also films on campus a weekly TV show that reaches by local cable about 16,000 homes. A 1½-hour feature film with full color, sound and music was also student-produced. Each year, artists at Forman choose a theme and paint a delightful 42-foot mural, which they hang in their otherwise nondescript dining hall.

Although the kids complain about the food, their menu fare is fine compared with school food elsewhere. A good salad bar and several entrees and desserts are available. Meals are served cafeteria-style in a clean, but rather crowded dining hall.

Not all of the faculty are certified in special education or learning disabilities, for the director feels that the school's training program is sufficient. Since no students are severely motor- or speech-impaired, adaptive physical education, sensory integration and speech therapy are not offered. Private speech instruction is available, and a part-time psychologist sees students for an extra fee. There is a high teacher turnover rate among Forman's primarily young and female staff, probably because of the low salary schedule.

Most students plan to attend college. In order to assure the best possible placement, Forman employs part-time college counselors who match colleges and students. These counselors know which programs offer the special support and counseling necessary for the academic success of LD students.

The achievement and effort grades given to students every two weeks determine admittance to "Green Key," an honor society recognizing "the ideal Formanite." Grades also determine whether a student's presence is required in supervised study hall. Comprehensive written reports and letter grades are sent home to parents twice a year. A fall parents' weekend and conferences arranged whenever desired keep home-school channels open.

Students appreciate what Forman provides. Typical comments heard include: "The teachers here really care." "It's like a family." "I'm learning something." "The food stinks." "There's too much homework." "It's not out in the boonies." "There aren't enough girls." Such are typical remarks from boys and girls at a top-notch regular boarding school.

THE GATEWAY SCHOOL OF NEW YORK   Private/Coed
921 Madison   Day
New York, NY 10021   Enrollment 30
      Ages 5-10

Since 1965, Gateway has been offering an excellent multifaceted remedial program for primary school-aged children in a church building on New York City's posh Upper East Side.

Currently, the main thrust of the program is the development of essential social skills. Follow-up studies on former students had revealed that though "graduates" were succeeding academically, they often were socially immature and awkward. Thus, the curriculum has been redesigned to emphasize "relating effectively to others." These social skills are, according to the director, the most complicated lessons an LD child must learn.

Two tiers of pink and cream-colored classrooms and offices surround a vaulted assembly area; in this sparkling common room the Gateway boys and girls, aged 5 to 10 years, spend an important part of their school day. Each morning during "Grandstand", all 30 students gather in this common room and learn such lessons as how to listen, how to follow directions, how to be truly polite and how to be a friend. The children are taught the nuances of body language and voice inflection. They learn to pick up cues from their teacher, to imitate movements and how to sequence through a step-by-step flag ceremony. Because children such as these so often take out their frustrations on one another through scapegoating, they are shown outlets for unhappy feelings. When the pledge of allegiance is finished, the children quietly put away their chairs and march off to classes.

The students know and follow their highly structured routine easily. The five morning classes of four to six pupils meet following Grandstand from 10 AM to noon for reading and adaptive physical education. The director is in charge of the reading program, which is eclectic but strongly influenced by the Orton-Gillingham method. Skill-oriented activities prescribed by the occupational therapist and optometrist, which usually involve work with coordination, vision, body awareness and balance, are practiced in the church gymnasium during adaptive physical education.

From noon to 12:30 PM, all eat the lunches they've brought from home. Underneath each lunch is a colorful placemat designed and decorated by one of the groups whose daily turn it was to do so. For half an hour after lunch, children either read in small groups or pass the time in unsupervised play, i.e., social interaction. This earned independent time with peers is designed to allow reinforcement of what was learned during the Grandstand period.

The afternoons are given over to team sports and games, storytelling, puppetry, music, art and social studies. Twice a week after school, Gateway's very active parents' association sponsors swimming classes in the church pool.

All teachers on the 15-member staff are certified in special education. They receive additional training at Gateway in optometrics and language and motor development. This allows the school's holistic therapeutic approach to be integrated by each teacher into each child's program. Thus, the language therapist might adjust her methods to accommodate a visual problem. The staff includes five classroom teachers, a psychologist, speech pathologist, transition teacher, a music specialist and consultants in math, occupational therapy and optometrics.

The specialists screen students and then fashion individual programs to be implemented during class or gym. The psychologist observes the children in the classrooms and advises teachers and parents. The speech pathologist works with small groups, as does a music teacher who comes twice a week. The latter has children use their motor, visual and auditory modalities to read music, sing and pound out rhythms on percussion instruments. The transition teacher's job is to smooth the way for Gateway departees in their subsequent schools. Student teachers occasionally help out at Gateway and reduce the overall teacher-pupil ratio to below one to two.

All of Gateway's students come from New York City or Westchester County. They are a diverse lot: the daily flag ceremony resembles a miniature United Nations assembly. The school's tuition is $8,600, but two thirds of the student body are funded. Admission is gained through a two-pronged evaluation consisting of classroom observation and a psychological evaluation. The school looks for children with low to above average intelligence who will be able to return to a regular classroom in two to four years. The staff meets with the parents to determine their willingness to be cooperative and supportive. Parents are encouraged to observe classes, meet in evening groups with the psychologist to discuss management techniques and confer with the teachers and specialists.

Problem solving is a major program emphasis at Gateway. "We don't give kids answers," the director states, "we want them to figure out solutions for themselves." At Gateway one never hears "Do this," but rather "How do you think this should be done?"

Gateway offers a special program for special youngsters. In enabling its students to think and learn and do for themselves, Gateway provides them with the priceless gift of self-reliance. By simultaneously building social and academic skills, the children receive the poise and foundations they need to develop long-lasting confidence in themselves.

STEPHEN GAYNOR SCHOOL *Private/Coed*
22 W. 74th Street *Day*
New York, NY 10023 *Enrollment 105*
 Ages 6-13

A sense of orderliness, a touch of class and a feeling of efficiency prevail in this trim and tidy converted mansion on New York City's elegant West Side.

The Stephen Gaynor School began operations as a day school in 1961 in a three-room apartment. Soon afterwards, the founders, Dr. Miriam Michael, Mrs. Yvette Siegel and Dr. Bert Schoeneman, decided to relocate at the present 74th Street address. All three are still involved in directing the school which now has an enrollment of 105 boys and girls between the ages of 6 and 12.

Gaynor offers these children a planned, structured and controlled environment with emphasis on the mastery of basic subjects. Its goal is to reintegrate each student successfully into the regular school system by the time he is 12 years old. In order to accomplish this objective, students are carefully screened and are then chosen on the basis of their potential to be mainstreamed. According to Dr. Michael, director of psychological services, 90 percent of Gaynor students do return to a regular school setting and most of the students eventually enter college.

The school is small; maximum enrollment is 120. Full use is made of all space; little nooks are turned into mini-classrooms just big enough for one student and a teacher. Normally there are eight children in a class, each of which is self-contained and has a head teacher and an assistant. Student teachers, primarily from Bank and Columbia Teachers Colleges, also take part in classroom activities.

The daily curriculum stresses the basic academic areas. Goals are clearly defined for each student, and a plan of systematic, sequential masteries is written into each program. The teaching pace is dictated by the student's learning pace so that each student can be rewarded with success with every application of effort. A multisensory approach is used to ensure mastery of academic skills. Distractions are kept at a minimum; visitors are not encouraged. One day for visits by professionals in the field is planned annually, though, and parent days are scheduled throughout the year.

The staff consists of 12 teachers, all of whom have Master's degrees in special education, and eight assistant teachers who are working on their Master's. In addition to the teaching staff, the faculty includes a psychologist, two remediation teachers and three language specialists, and there are teachers for shop, gym, music, art and typing as well. Computers are budgeted for 1984. Facilities for woodworking, typing and art are not large, but efficient use is made of what is provided. The art room is noteworthy for the extensive variety of equipment and the resultant opportunities to experiment with different media.

Students make use of the nearby "Y," Central Park and the small gym at the school for their physical education program. Training in gross motor development and participation by the athletically able in structured, controlled, competitive games are the principal objectives. Regular trips to nearby museums are another extramural must. Most students are well-acquainted with the logistics of getting around a big city. Some commute via the subway, for there are stations of two subway lines nearby. Others, since they are eligible by virtue of residing within city limits, use bus transportation provided by the New York City Board of Education.

Admission to Gaynor is dependent upon the director's receipt of all records and test results and an on-site interview. If data are not complete, additional testing may be required. Tuition for the academic year is $8,000. There are a limited number of scholarships available, but no funding is received from the city or state.

Parents who want for their children a highly structured, well-ordered academic environment in which extensive remediation is incorporated would do well to check out the Stephen Gaynor School, particularly if they wish their progeny to attend college.

THE GOW SCHOOL
South Wales, NY 14139

Private/Boys
Residential
Enrollment 132
Ages 12-20

The 132 junior and senior high school boys who attend the Gow School experience total learning immersion. Classes begin at 8:20 AM, Monday through Friday, and continue until 6 PM, with one and one-half hours of this time devoted to athletics. After dinner, the boys have a half hour reading period and a mandatory two-hour supervised study hall to complete homework assigned during the day. On Saturday, classes are held until 1 PM. Success is virtually guaranteed, as almost all boys enroll in college after graduation. According to a recent study by Johns Hopkins University, 60 percent of a sampling of 600 graduates earned bachelor's degrees and nearly 10 percent gained advanced degrees. About half of the college graduates are working in jobs at the managerial level; almost 20 percent are in professional or technical careers such as architecture, engineering and teaching; 15 percent became salesmen. The survey also revealed that two thirds now read for pleasure, and only 12 percent still consider reading a chore. "Most of our alumni have gone into disciplines that require reading. They have not all become forest rangers and hermits," states headmaster David Gow.

One of the reasons for this success is that the Gow School is very selective in its admissions procedure. An average to above IQ, as demonstrated through a two-day assessment at the school, is required for entrance. The fee for this comprehensive evaluation is a low $115. In the required on-campus interview with the staff, the boy must also demonstrate whether "his education can be advanced by the school and whether he gives promise of making a successful adjustment to the work and life of the school."

For those chosen (the school has a waiting list), the tuition is a modest $9,100. This fee does not include laundry, books, school supplies or athletic apparel. These extra costs are estimated at $600. Limited scholarship assistance is available, but the school has no U.S.-funded students. Many students from Canada have tuition reimbursement, but Gow finds American school districts will not pay for outside placement because they feel they can handle these students themselves.

The living quarters at Gow are rather Spartan and bleak — but that's okay because little student time is spent lounging around the dorms. "We use them only for sleeping," states one boy. Almost all staff, as well as the headmaster, live on campus, and there is a master in every dorm. When inspected, all dorms were exceptionally neat and clean, and all had adequate storage space. For those who have earned the privilege through exemplary behavior and good grades, honor dorms in married masters' homes provide a more relaxed, less structured, personal environment. However, all follow the daily schedule of the school. Everyone eats together in the large dining hall, where meals are served family-style by a master at the head of each table. Boys look forward to receiving "care packages" from home, however, for while the meals here are adequate, there are few leftovers and no night-time snacks to further satisfy teenage boys' voracious appetites.

The boys don't seem to miss "dorm life," so busy are they with classes, study halls and athletics. Free time is spent in the newly constructed library/reading room and gymnasium/activities center. The former contains a large stone fireplace, comfortable seating, an audio-visual center, photography darkroom, study carrels, 7,000 books, many magazines and open space for 11,000 volumes. The gymnasium/activities center contains a full high school basketball court with six baskets, a tennis court, space for volleyball, badminton and other court sports, and a raised stage for drama productions.

Extracurricular activities vary, depending on student interest and faculty expertise. According to the associate headmaster, a club will be formed if there is sufficient interest; he himself sponsors the riding club. The school has a yearbook and chess, photography, outing and glee clubs. All boys are encouraged to participate in the two yearly plays. Cultural trips to nearby Buffalo also take place.

Gow was founded in 1926 to "investigate and find by observation and research better solutions to the problems of scholastic failure in boys of high school and junior high school age." This makes Gow the oldest school in the country to have a continuous program of its kind. Peter Gow, the founder, had encountered in his teaching "many students who were troubled by mysterious difficulties in school work wholly out of proportion to their obvious alertness and competence in practical life situations." The school early began a program of "reconstructive language" therapy (RL) which now forms the core of the Gow curriculum.

The reconstructive language class that every boy takes six days a week uses an Orton Gillingham approach, which stresses phonics, syllabics, oral reading, vocabulary development and spelling. The class is taught by Mr. Gow and other long-time teachers who have been trained in this method.

In addition to reconstructive language, each boy follows a curriculum similar to that found in a traditional college preparatory school. Small classes of from one to eight follow a round table format; lecture and discussion techniques are used almost exclusively. Courses include English, geography, world history, U.S. history, economics, research skills, mathematics, science, French, German, Latin, and Spanish. A class of 15 seniors studies "research skills," taught by the associate headmaster, specifically designed to develop skills needed at college.

Students at Gow are not emotionally or physically disabled; no psychological or formal counseling services, no sensory integration, no adaptive education or speech therapy courses are offered. This doesn't mean that boys do not receive counseling; plenty of "cottage counseling" is available from the masters and headmaster, all of whom live on campus and really get to know the boys and their problems.

Physical education is mandatory for each boy each day. Sports include a wide variety of both intramural and interscholastic activities. Offered are lacrosse, cross country skiing and running, soccer, tennis, downhill skiing on the school's own ski hill, basketball in the gymnasium and softball on one of the school's athletic fields. The sports program is considered vital; every boy must participate. Rule learning, group interaction and frustration reduction, rather than winning, are the goals of the program.

Although these boys are basically able to develop and maintain good peer and adult relationships, weekly classes in interpersonal relationships are required. The school calls this a course in character; it is structured to improve a boy's self-image and self-confidence. Learning to think on one's feet and a certain degree of poise are attained by addressing large groups. Emphasis is also placed on appreciating the feelings of others. The course is taught by the headmaster and is highly regarded by students and faculty.

Parents are invited to the school for a weekend in May and are welcome at any time during the year. Boys are graded numerically at the end of every marking period, and a comprehensive written evaluation is sent to parents at the end of each term.

It is the associate headmaster's task to find appropriate post-graduate placement for his students. Mark Kimball, who has been with the school for eight years, is in touch with or has personal acquaintance with many suitable college programs for his students. He meets with students and their parents during their senior year, and off campus visits are arranged.

The staff of male masters maintain excellent control of all classes. Discipline problems are just not evident. There are no "quiet rooms" or behavioral assistants at Gow. Gow does not require that its teachers have special education credentials; they look for men who like and understand boys, are willing to live on campus and devote a great portion of their time to their charges and are firmly grounded in their academic speciality. Mr. Gow and the veteran teachers train new staff members.

Research into the origin and remediation of dyslexia continues. But until some miraculous cure is found, the reconstructive teaching method that Gow and other schools like it employ, is a nonpareil way to change inadequacies into proficiencies.

LANDMARK SCHOOL
Prides Crossing, MA 01965

Private/Coed
Day/Residential
Enrollment 388
Ages 8-21

If the qualities looked for in an educational institution include a wide range of challenging programs, a stimulating social environment and fine academic instruction, Landmark may well be one of the best of its kind in the country.

With its four campuses and 388 students, Landmark has advantages common to a large school in the same way that a large city offers experiences different from those of a small town. Yet, according to its headmaster, Dr. Charles Drake, who founded the school in 1969, the school works very hard to maintain a family-like atmosphere.

The school offers many choices. Individual program selection is determined not so much by which alternative is superior as by which alternative is preferred by the student. Should one feel the urge to travel the Greek Islands or meet the "Tall Ships" in France or sail the North American waterways, then a year aboard the *Te Vega*, the school's 156 foot gaff-rigged schooner, might be the right choice. If students decide to tackle the college scene but feel the need to "brush up" on skills, they might want to enroll in Landmark's college-prep program. When students are ready to return to mainstream education at the secondary level, they will probably attend transition classes which approximate those of the traditional high school. Another option on a separate campus is for children with expressive language difficulties. Of course, there are also the regular elementary and high school programs which are geared to remediation and an eventual return to a regular classroom. Tuition for all boarders during the regular year is $17,150; for day students it is $9,500.

Three of the four Massachusetts schools (another is located in Los Angeles, California) — the one for special language, the elementary and the high school — operate out of one-time summer mansions formerly owned by the Boston aristocracy. The transition class and the college preparatory program have spacious quarters in a rented former school building. The mansions overlook the ocean and have magnificent views of historic Salem and Marblehead on the Massachusetts Bay. The rich culture of Boston is but a 25-mile hop away, while the quaint, bustling fishing port of Gloucester is just around the corner. Aside from the view and the rather faded beauty of the old mansions, the campuses are not really picturesque. No attempt has been made to develop any architectural continuity, a fact which has resulted in a scattered, unaesthetic hodgepodge of buildings, some of which look like leftover army barracks. Many of the rooms badly need a good paint job. The dormitories are crowded, often with six in one room. Meals are served cafeteria-style, and little attempt at elegance or etiquette is made.

These unappealing features should be overlooked, for the Landmark program has much else to recommend it. The program is intended for bright, dyslexic children of normal or above intelligence. The 324 boys and 64 girls come from 28 states and 13 foreign countries. The core of the teaching program is a one-to-one session with a tutor each day. Major emphasis is placed on the development of language skills — speech, reading, writing and spelling. Other important areas covered in the curriculum include motor, auditory and visual training, math, typing, social studies, science and computer training. Classes are small, ungraded and arranged according to the child's ability and age.

Development of skills and competencies outside of the classroom is a vital part of the whole program. An outdoor "confidence course" is designed to develop motor coordination and self-assurance in group situations. The athletic program offers a variety of seasonal sports, as well as regular junior and senior high intramural programs. The school has an indoor swimming pool and organizes extensive weekend trips for backpacking, camping, canoeing and skiing.

An exceptional feature of the Landmark School is its Watermark program, which lets students participate in an unusual, exciting sailing adventure. As participants in Watermark, students learn all aspects of ship operation: navigation, seamanship, rowing, and line and sail handling. Students share all responsibilities of group living, such as food preparations, daily chores and ship maintenance. The Watermark program is a seven-week summer program for boys and girls between the ages of 8 and 18. Students attend academic classes each morning and learn seamanship and sailing skills during the afternoon.

The ship, *Te Vega*, operates all year long as a floating school. While exploring such places as the Grecian Islands, Denmark, France and North America, the students carry on their basic academic courses and tutorials - with special emphasis on marine biology.

Landmark offers vocational training. The primary purpose is not to train for a job, but rather to master fine motor skills. The elementary school offers a woodworking and small engine repair shop. The high school has courses in carpentry, automechanics, printing, graphic arts and computer programming. The carpentry elective is outstanding. Some students have built a structure for extra classrooms, dorm rooms and the new science laboratory. Other students are building small boats to be used in the Watermark program.

Two other extra-special offerings of the Landmark Schools are its transition and post-graduate programs. The transition school is patterned after the curricula of traditional schools. The students are graded, classes are larger, and there are no tutorials. The goal of the program is to integrate the specific skills acquired thus far and to utilize these constructively in the larger classroom. The post-graduate program, in interesting and seemingly successful experiment, is designed to give those who are potentially college bound the skills they need. The curriculum includes the tutorial as well as classes in composition, language arts, mathematics and computer literacy. Emphasis is placed upon the students' organizational and study skills.

Landmark believes that its special way of working with the dyslexic child is successful, and it wishes to share its knowledge and experience with others. To this end an outreach program has been developed. Outreach operates as a consulting service. Through workshops, special presentations and on-site training, teachers outside of the Landmark community become acquainted with its methods.

The staff at Landmark is large and competent. In addition to the 118 members of the teaching staff, all of whom have been trained in a Landmark version of the Orton-Gillingham approach, the school maintains a full-time vocational counselor and a school placement counselor whose job it is to find proper future school placement for all youngsters leaving Landmark, whether they are of elementary or college age.

A commentary on Landmark is incomplete without making mention of Dr. Charles Drake, the school's founder and headmaster. A recognized leader in the field of learning disabilities, Drake has a special affinity with his students, for he is also dyslexic. Whenever major disciplinary action is required, Drake acts as the student's advocate. With a doctoral degree from Harvard, Drake serves as a living example to the boys and girls at Landmark. He overcame. So also can they.

LINDEN HILL SCHOOL
South Mountain Rd.
Northfield, MA 01360

Private/Boys
Residential
Enrollment 30
Ages 10-14

A jewel of a school, little Linden Hill, located high in the hills on 110 wooded acres overlooking the Connecticut River, looks and feels like home. Daily life here more closely resembles that of a family than a residential institution. Boys sit around in a comfortable living room, eat in a dining room and perform such household chores as washing dishes. "Why not?" queries the headmaster. "This is their home."

Orderliness and organization are valued at Linden Hill. Typically, adolescent boys' quarters are usually disaster areas, but these small, twin dormitory rooms would amaze moms: clothes are hung-up, shoes are lined-up, beds are neatly made-up. Meals are served, not cafeteria-style, but in a dining room replete with white tablecloths, cloth napkins and formal place settings. A teacher sits at each table and in a low-keyed, joking manner ensures that the boys mind their manners and eat their "veggies". A short thanksgiving prefaces meals prepared by a cook who obviously loves his position. The menu stresses good nutrition: no salt or sugar is available at the table; fresh fruit is served for dessert. But, once a week, the boys may indulge in the their beloved "junk food."

The main school building, a quaint Victorian-style farmhouse built circa 1835, houses the administration offices, the headmaster's and faculty apartments, the kitchen, dining and living rooms. Just inside the back hall, 30 pairs of slippers neatly await 30 pairs of muddy feet, allowing the boys to pad around their farmhouse in Japanese fashion. The living room, used as a common room, provides a home-like atmosphere; comfortable couches and easy chairs surround a grand old fireplace. Even without a fire burning, a real warmth radiates throughout this well-preserved building.

Classrooms, a science laboratory, library, small gym and study hall/auditorium are located in Haskell Hall behind the main building. The school also has a woodworking shop in the basement of the dormitory building.

Academically, the students thrive at Linden Hill. The boys dress for school in coat and tie to emphasize that learning is serious business. The reading program is based upon the Orton-Gillingham, step-by-step, sequential approach to acquiring language. Teachers, although not necessarily formally trained in special education, are well-versed in this teaching method. The school is small enough for each of the eight faculty members to become well-acquainted with the special needs of each of the 30 boys. Classes are exceptionally small, averaging from one to four pupils. The standard academic program of mathematics, science, literature, history, geography and composition is required of each boy. An interesting feature is that in the basic content courses, such as geography, history and science, all the classes, beginner to advanced, study the same topics at the same time. Thus, educational field trips can be planned for the whole school, and each boy will have some frame of reference.

Students are carefully selected for admission to ensure that newcomers fit into the homogeneous student body. All boys participate simultaneously as a group in all extracurricular activities. For this reason, as well as the dictates of space, the school accepts only 30 dyslexic boys, aged 10 to 14, of average or above intelligence. No overt acting-out or behavior problems can be accommodated. The school has a full enrollment and has had to turn away many qualified students for lack of space. Tuition is $12,700.

In addition to the academic program, non-graded classes are offered in art, music, photography, model building and woodshop. Maple syrup making is a frenetic activity when the sap runs as the boys work in shifts around the clock to make enough for the dining table and for gifts.

Everyone participates in the several dramatic productions held each year. Such spoofs as "Robin Good and His Merry Hoods" and "Camel Lot" undoubtedly nurture many latent dramatic talents.

The school holds to the philosophy that "lots of good exercise is vital for the proper development of a young man, and skill in athletics also helps to develop a boy's self-confidence." The boys are required to train in several sports each semester; soccer, judo, horseback riding, skiing, swimming, baseball, tennis and track are offered. It also seems that everyone brings a bicycle and hiking shoes to school. The entire student body belongs to Linden Hill's interscholastic soccer team, which plays eight or nine of the area's private schools. Everyone on the team plays every game. Naturally, with this "no bench sitting" philosophy, the team does not win very often, but the team's spirit is high, and so is its sense of sportsmanship.

The Linden Hill faculty talk very positively: they speak in terms of what the student has accomplished in class, not in terms of what he has yet to learn. Once a boy has reached grade level, it is time for him to move on. The headmaster, like any good father, will review the different schools in which the child is interested and offer his advice. The following year, he will contact the new school to see how his former student is progressing. Linden Hill, truly a gentleman's school, offers more than a good education. It offers a good life.

THE PATHWAY SCHOOL
Box 18
Audubon, PA 19407

Private/Coed
Residential
Enrollment 125
Ages 5-18

Since 1961, the Pathway School has been doing an excellent job of working with youngsters between 5 and 18 years of age who have severe learning disabilities, behavior problems, normal or below intelligence and speech impairments.

The staff is as extensive as the school is expensive. Tuition ranges from $24,000 for students who board for 11 months to $11,750 for nine-month day students. Most of the school's 125 boys and girls are funded by their school districts. The teaching staff is composed of 11 fully certified LD teachers and 11 assistants, one art and music teacher, two adaptive physical education instructors, three career education persons and speech and reading specialists. An educational director and separate principals for the elementary and high school administer the educational program. A clinical staff of five psychologists, one social worker and two behavioral assistants provide counseling.

Each child has regular individual and group therapy. Crisis counseling is available instantly as some of the students are "borderline psychotic." Dr. Donald Painting, the clinical director, is also experimenting with biofeedback techniques in behavior control. Pathway endeavors to coordinate juvenile psychotherapy with parent counseling. For the boarding student's parents, these sessions are not easily arranged; frequent telephone contact between parents and counselors is substituted.

A thorough prescriptive diagnostic evaluation is administered prior to enrollment to determine if the Pathway program will be appropriate for a particular child. Upon acceptance, a completely personalized program is devised for each enrollee based upon the assessed educational and behavioral strengths and weaknesses. Achievement levels and social/emotional development determine homeroom assignments. Here, students are instructed in English, reading, mathematics, and "Basic Living Skills." The high school students leave their homerooms for social studies, science, physical education and elective courses; elementary students remain in the self-contained classrooms.

Small classes with no more than 12 students are managed by a certified special education teacher and an assistant. Daily, morning teacher conferences enable the staff to work as a team to solve day-to-day classroom dilemmas. The teachers work individually or with small groups; each child works at his own rate. The atmosphere within classrooms is surprisingly industrious, considering the severity of the learning and behavioral problems of the youngsters; the students remain "on task." On call are two behavioral assistants to minister to those children who might become disruptive in the classroom. They have some "quiet time" together in one of the two rooms provided for that purpose.

Supplemental programs in adaptive physical education, speech, language and reading development are a part of the Pathway experience. The school has a small gym and ample outdoor space for field sports; in 1983, Pathway competed in basketball and softball against three other area schools. Three speech pathologists provide therapy for individual students in articulation, receptive and expressive language development, voice and fluency. A resource room teacher gives supplemental reading instruction on an individual basis to recommended students. Art and music programs are offered once a week. Instructional kits are used to teach basic life skills. Students follow step-by-step instructions to bake a cake or repair a small motor. Tasks become progressively more difficult, but the child can set his own pace. A sense of accomplishment, once the project is finished, is its own reward.

Career education at Pathway goes beyond book learning. Students go from the classroom into the work force where they are exposed to a host of jobs. Currently, students are serving apprenticeships at auto body shops, riding stables, bookstores, hospitals, a nursery and print shop.

Along with on-the-job career exploration, introductory career awareness kits give students "hands on" occupational experiences with job related tools and equipment. Counseling concerning the student's job aptitude and preference is a vital part of this program. Career education also teaches the student what is required of a good employee.

Another noteworthy specialized program has been developed for those students who lack high school graduation credits and want to prepare for the General Education Development (GED) tests.

Residential cottages, scattered around the pleasant, 13-acre Pathway campus, provide boarders with a home-like atmosphere. From 12 to 17 youngsters of like ages and social maturity, under the supervision of the live-in cottage leader and three residential counselors, prepare meals together, garden together and probably even fight a little. The counselors show genuine concern for the social, intellectual and emotional well-being of their charges. A behavior modification program attempts to facilitate peaceful cohabitation and to motivate academic achievement. Points can be gained for successfully completing predetermined academic tasks or demonstrating acceptable social behavior. These points, when totaled, can be cashed in for an appropriate reward.

Kids have fun at Pathway. Numerous afternoon and evening activities, intramural sports, scouting, overnights and community projects are all part of Pathway's highly structured plan and philosophy. Students' time, especially that of the younger ones, is fully planned. However, "free time" is offered as a reward to high school students.

Boys and girls with deficient social skills, behavior problems, severe communicative disorders and moderate to severe learning disabilities feel comfortable but challenged in the warm, caring, but achievement-oriented environment at Pathway. Pathway's interdisciplinary team concept is well suited to meet their needs.

PINE RIDGE SCHOOL
1075 Williston Rd.
Williston, VT 05495

Private/Coed
Residential
Enrollment 88
Ages 12-18

Boys and girls at Pine Ridge are guided by the firm and loving hands of a couple of well-seasoned grandfather types who have been with this school since it was first established in 1968. "Hoppy" and "Chuck", as they are called by faculty and students alike, are determined to develop responsibility and self-confidence in their charges. To this end, the 88 boys and girls in residence, whose ages range from 12 to 18, are expected to make many of their own decisions and, once made, to carry through with them.

The school is located on a restful, rural, 100-acre site at the foot of the Green Mountains of Vermont. Only eight miles away is Burlington, the state's largest city, and Pine Ridge makes good use of the advantages of its urban neighbor.

An air of casualness surrounds the place. Teachers and students are on a first-name basis, and there is no dress code, either written or unwritten, for staff or students. If this sometimes manifests itself in a rather unkempt look, it is all a part of a plan. The directors have found that such informality offers the students welcome relief from all the other rules and regulations they must follow in this highly structured educational institution.

The major emphasis of schooling at Pine Ridge is the nurturing of both the intellectual and the physical growth of its students. To meet this goal, the school employs two complete, well-qualified staffs, one for the academic and one for the residential programs. Annual tuition costs for the residential school year are $15,000.

The core of the academic program is a daily, one-to-one remedial language tutorial which is taught by tutors trained in the Orton-Gillingham method. Each tutorial is individually designed following an assessment of the student's processing and language skills. The tutorial is backed up by a skills laboratory assignment during which time students work in small groups to master those skills introduced in the tutorials. Tutors are supervised by the tutorial director who keeps close track of all student progress.

Regular classwork in English, science and social studies is offered at three levels — foundation, intermediate and advanced. For these courses students are grouped according to ability. An impressive mathematics program offers courses in computer training, trigonometry and pre-calculus to those who demonstrate a strong mathematical aptitude. Students write an annual research paper for which they go to the public libraries nearby, as the school maintains no library of its own. Informal after-school instruction is given in photography, woodworking and automechanics. Supervised evening study hall is required except for those who have shown they can manage without surveillance.

All teachers and tutors hold college degrees; classroom teachers are certified in their specialty. For those needing the special Orton-Gillingham training, it is provided in an intensive seven-week internship held at the school each summer.

The physical education program is an important feature of the student's total educational experience. Very few athletic facilities are located on school premises. Pine Ridge has found it advantageous to maintain little and provide much. The physical education classes are held on and off campus five days per week from 3:10 to 4:30 in the afternoon. Pine Ridge purchases memberships to clubs which offer tennis, racquetball, physical conditioning and swimming. The local armory serves as a gymnasium. Coeducational soccer and basketball teams play teams from other area schools. The students are provided with passes for downhill ski classes at a private ski area run by the Cochran family of Olympic fame. The hockey team rents private ice time. Students with motor coordination difficulties take a special adaptive physical education program.

Six qualified instructors monitor and direct the physical education classes. Students pick an activity suitable for the season and participate in it for eleven weeks. Once students have made their choice, they can't switch and are responsible for finishing the course.

Two joint, five-day outdoor camping trips are planned for faculty and students. Emphasis here is on developing cooperative group skills. The winter expedition takes places in a cabin located on the school grounds. In the spring, biking, hiking or canoeing trips are planned.

Housing is arranged with primary consideration being given to age and compatibility factors. Girls reside in the main building, a former country inn, which houses the administrative offices. Boys live in two off-campus houses and three campus facilities. Dormitories have common living rooms and very small bedrooms which sleep two. One boy jokingly referred to his room situation as "living in a closet and sleeping on a shelf." When visited, the rooms were all neat and clean. The single dining room serves truly delicious, cafeteria-style meals.

Pine Ridge works with children who have all sorts of learning disabilities and does not rely strictly upon test scores as the basis for admission. As the school does not have a diagnostic staff or employ a psychologist, prior testing before admission is required. The school tries not to accept students with emotional or behavioral problems, but should such problems occur the staff is more than willing to walk that extra mile with any child who they think can be helped by their program. Close to 60 percent of the school's graduates go on to college.

An education at Pine Ridge is designed as an antidote to earlier, unpleasant school experiences. Three features set this school apart—its great sports program, its beautiful setting and its academics. A former student who went on to complete his schooling elsewhere summed up his experience at Pine Ridge by saying, "I really enjoyed it there."

RIVERVIEW SCHOOL
Rt. 6A
East Sandwich, MA 02537

Private/Coed
Residential
Enrollment 110
Ages 12-20

An exemplary school for the less academically able boy or girl, Riverview has just celebrated its Silver Anniversary and has every intention to continue serving the learning disabled. The school has changed focus throughout the years, but, for the past 13, it has concentrated on helping students from ages 12 to 20 with "multiple minimal handicaps." If they could be handled separately, these handicaps would pose relatively minor adjustment difficulties, but the existence of several of these disabilities within one child compounds academic and social problems.

Riverview is dedicated to developing not only the academic potential of its students, but their social awareness as well. These two components are considered vital to independent and productive membership in society. Riverview's commitment to help its students achieve this goal is accomplished by creating separate, unique programs for all students. IEPs are designed to challenge and ensure success. Riverview literally maintains 110 programs for 110 students.

Many of the 25 teachers are well-seasoned veterans. All are credentialed in both special education and their subject area. They instruct students in small groups of six to ten on Riverview's 19-acre campus in beautiful, historic Cape Cod. The atmosphere of the Cape has enticed many a teacher from large school districts elsewhere. The students profit from the low teacher-turnover rate; seeing familiar faculty faces at the beginning of a new school year is especially reassuring to youngsters like those at Riverview, many of whom return for five or six years. A speech therapist, five reading specialists, two school psychologists, adaptive physical educators and art and music teachers augment the teaching staff.

The curriculum includes courses in English, mathematics, social studies, computer science, independent or small group reading tutorials, speech therapy, art, music, homemaking, office practices and industrial arts. The staff evaluates the student's progress and performance tri-annually, and a written narrative along with letter grades is sent home to parents.

The reading program at Riverview can vary from an individual reading tutorial three hours per week to an extra, small-group reading class to no extra reading remediation. While Riverview incorporates a combination of remedial reading approaches, the Orton-Gillingham influence is evident. Even the most avid of readers at Riverview could not possibly exhaust the available material in the beautiful 4,000 volume library/multimedia center. The magazine collection alone, with everything from *The Smithsonian* to *Sports Illustrated* could entertain a child for weeks.

The school's prevocational department is exceptional. Students learn to function independently in life situations. In a well-equipped homemaking laboratory, students study food preparation, textiles, grooming, child care and related home living skills. The large industrial arts building has separate classrooms for mechanical drawing, small engine repair, bicycle and home repair, printing and woodworking. The career arts building is arranged like an office with desks, filing cabinets, typewriters and steno notebooks. One of the four new computers is employed in the office practices program. All seniors work off campus one half day each week at a local business or social agency. For an additional $2,000, students can spend four afternoons per week at a local vocational/technical school. A vocational guidance course familiarizes students with and helps them choose between career options. A post-graduate program allows many to attend the local community college or vocational school while continuing to study at Riverview.

The staff maintains good communication with colleges, specialized programs and vocational institutions in order to ensure proper placement of graduates. The career counselors consider the child's interest, his continuing progress and his potential when recommending career options. For the past four years, the school has sent questionnaires to its graduates, and success stories have been plentiful. Some former students have bachelor's degrees, most are in the working world and a few have their own businesses. One former student is presently being considered for the Riverview Board of Directors.

After-school and evening activities are a major part of Riverview life. An activities director structures the extracurricular and residential program to provide an environment conducive to the development of "good personal hygiene, domestic skills, and mature personal relations." Every weekend, there is a chaperoned trip to Hyannis for several hours of free time. On Sunday afternoons, the school takes field trips to cultural and historic sites in Boston and on the Cape. The students are not left on their own; there is always adult leadership to provide the structure this type of youngster needs. With the same number of boys and girls, a monthly school dance, a spring prom and informal dorm parties enable students to feel comfortable and to relate appropriately with the opposite sex. Riverview has an equal number of boys and girls enrolled.

The absence of children with severe emotional difficulties allows Riverview teenagers to enjoy a regular coeducational high school environment. The boys' basketball games have female cheerleaders; there are over 30 organizations and sports clubs to join. In fact, shown any significant curiosity, Riverview is delighted to introduce its teens to new fields of interests. The staff feels one of the great strengths of its program is its emphasis upon social development and group interaction.

Competitive sports are not emphasized at Riverview, although basketball, soccer and softball teams do play against a few local schools. Individual sports such as cross country skiing, running and swimming are designed to improve physical coordination. The school has athletic playing fields and a fully equipped gymnasium for daily physical education and extracurricular sports activities.

A separate staff of 18 child care workers, all certified by the New England Association for Child Care, manage the residential duties, and a registered nurse is on duty at all times. All boys are housed on campus in two dormitories. One of these, brand new in 1983, is simply spectacular. Housing 30 boys, this dorm has a large common room with a kitchen for weekend and evening snacking, two separate living rooms, good art on the walls, sturdy comfortable furniture, live plants and carpeted floors. The bedrooms for two are organized and well kept with ample drawer space, desks, adequate lighting and extra room for the inevitable stereos, hobbies and collections. The second boys' dorm offers the same amenities but pales somewhat in comparison to its flashier counterpart. In both male dorms a live-in married couple provides a touch of home-like living. Girls live with a house mother in either an on-campus dormitory or in one of four houses located about a mile away. The girls, it seems, try to vie with each other to see who can gather the largest collection of stuffed animals.

Meals are served cafeteria-style in a large, pleasant dining room. The food is good and healthy. A salad bar, lots of fruit and a soup-of-the-day are all served with the entrèe; seconds are encouraged, and milk is plentiful. A blessing is said before the meal, and a teacher sits at each table with a small group of students.

Riverview does not have a diagnostic clinic. All students must have a previous diagnostic workup showing identifiable learning disabilities and no primary emotional problems. Following receipt of available diagnostic information, a personal interview is arranged for those students for whom the program seems appropriate. Upon admittance, all students are screened for reading and speech difficulties, and achievement tests are administered. Standardized achievement tests are administered each spring. Letter grades and written narrative reports are sent to parents three times per year. Individual parent conferences, either by telephone or personal visit, can be scheduled at the parent's convenience. Tuition at Riverview is $17,500 per year.

Riverview believes that the child with learning problems can lead a productive life as a contributing member of society. To accomplish this, Riverview builds self-confidence and develops social and academic skills so that a student upon leaving "will be able to realize his or her fullest potential for being a wholesome, realistic and mature individual."

WINDWARD SCHOOL	*Private/Coed*
Windward Ave.	*Day*
White Plains, NY 10605	*Enrollment 125*
	Ages 5-18

An excellent and experienced staff is the outstanding feature of Windward Day School. Each of the 45 teachers and five administrators has earned at least a Master's degree in special education and often possesses another comparable or more advanced degree. Even most of the assistant teachers either have or are working toward a graduate degree.

In addition to the classroom teachers, the staff includes three full-time remedial specialists who see children on a one-to-one basis, a full-time language and speech pathologist, a clinical psychologist and a psychiatric social worker.

This staff, versed as it is in the full panoply of remediation techniques, is not tied to a single methodology but is given *carte blanche* to mix and match whatever theories and practices are right for each child. Integrating a variety of remedial techniques is called the "eclectic approach." At Windward, unlike the practice elsewhere, this does not mean stumbling around looking for something that works. It means knowing what works. As one veteran teacher put it, "We are able to be more individualistic in our approach, and, because we are highly trained and experienced, we make fewer mistakes."

The 125 member Windward student body, which ranges from kindergarten through high school age, is drawn mostly from Westchester County, New York; Fairfield County, Connecticut; New York City and Long Island. Only those students from Westchester are provided transportation. Students from other areas rely upon various carpools or privately engaged busing services.

Requirements for admission to the school are that the child be diagnosed learning disabled and have average or above scores on intelligence tests. Because the school does not accept severely learning disabled or emotionally handicapped children, no New York State funding is available. Tuition for the 1983-1984 school year is $8,190 for kindergarten through 6th grade, $8,390 for 7th and 8th, and $8,850 for 9th through 12th.

Classrooms are large, bright and airy; their walls are covered with the children's essays, individual projects and art works. In addition to its academic offerings, Windward offers physical education, art, health, library skills and woodworking. An excellent library, staffed by a qualified librarian, is loaded with books and equipment. The library skills program is unique in that it is taught in tandem with the social studies program in order to develop research skills. The physical education program takes place in a small gymnasium and offers activities ranging from basic motor skills work to interscholastic team sports.

A new addition is being planned for the school as part of a 1983 renovation project. The building of four new classrooms will enable the high school to move out of the basement to brighter, perhaps more inspiring quarters. A new art room and a library media center are also to be added.

In 1984, Windward will graduate its first high school class. Presumably the school will have been successful in obtaining Board of Regents approval for its diploma.

Windward endeavers to model its academic structure on that of the finest prep schools. Its goal is to prepare its students to return to regular educational placement within two years. Homerooms are the nucleus around which the 8:30 AM to 2:30 PM school day is structured. Two teachers and no more than ten students are in self-contained elementary classrooms. The junior high and high school are departmentalized. All children have a daily, double period of reading-language in their homerooms. Groupings for math and social studies are determined according to skill and ability. A special "time out" room exists for the student whose teacher thinks he needs to get away from the classroom for awhile. In this retreat, the child gets help and counseling from a qualified and caring staff member.

The lovely, weathered brick Windward school building is located on six acres in a quiet, residential neighborhood of White Plains, New York. Windward looks and feels more like a private mansion than an institution. Each student, upon arrival, is treated as a welcome guest. This thoughtful attention is continued throughout his stay at Windward. Upon leaving, one of the staff will personally accompany the child and his parents to whichever school it has been determined he should next attend.

WINSTON PREPARATORY SCHOOL
4 West 76th Street
New York, NY 10023

Private/Coed
Day
Enrollment 50
Ages 13-18

Fifty boys and girls from a variety of ethnic backgrounds attend this "bare bones school," so lacking in the amenities that the kids' fund raising money went to buy a drinking fountain. This is hardly alarming since many special schools began in humble quarters only to move shortly thereafter to more spacious and appealing settings. The present church basement facilities certainly lack elegance, but the faculty and students believe that the quality of education found in their classrooms is what counts.

Winston Prep was founded in 1981 at the urging of New York City parents who wanted an academically oriented program for learning disabled adolescents unready to fit into the high school mainstream. Students of average or above intelligence, who have been identified by a diagnostic evaluation as LD and whose acting out is manageable, are eligible for admission. Roberta Michaels, a former assistant principal of the Stephen Gaynor School, is Winston Prep's director/founder. Her extensive experience has enabled her to identify and hand pick students for admission to her program.

Most students feel lucky to be at Winston; for many this is their last chance. Although the school's goal is to return the child to the mainstream with the knowledge and skill to "make it," for those who stay on Winston offers a state approved high school diploma. Not all of its students aspire to or are qualified for college, but many do go. Parents and teachers work together to ensure that the best and most realistic future school placement is found. Tuition is $7,900.

The staff is young, and all but the physical education teacher are female. All classroom teachers are experienced in learning disabilities and certified in special education. Assistant teachers are all college graduates, and many are enrolled in graduate school. The teaching staff is augmented by part-time interns from metropolitan area universities. An impressive support staff includes reading and math specialists, a speech and language pathologist, a consulting librarian and a psychologist.

Nine different reading and math classes and a special class for young people with expressive language difficulties enable all to be properly placed according to their skill levels. No more than ten students are in a class; in each, emphasis is upon age-appropriate instruction with concurrent remediation in areas of difficulty.

Space is utilized to the maximum at Winston. Tutorials are held in the hallways, and it is not uncommon to have several classes in one room. No one appears to be bothered by distractions around them; students and teachers alike are focused upon their tasks. There are only four regular classrooms; a small art room does double duty as a math class. Physical education classes are held two or three times per week in the church gym or at Central Park. A rather inadequate library houses the school's two computers.

New York City offers an abundance of outside-the-classroom resources to Winston preppies. Besides taking advantage of Central Park, the museums and other cultural activities, Winston has associated with one of the city's greatest educational institutions, Columbia Teachers College. A computer program was developed with Columbia in 1983, and ten students attended classes at the college's micro-computer lab. These students are now instructing their peers at Winston in the use of computers.

Two ingredients work in combination to insure the success of this fledgling school: a talented and hard working staff who teach their charges "not to accept failure but adopt strategies for success" and students who meet their educational challenges in a no-nonsense, determined and hard working way.

VILLA MARIA EDUCATION CENTER
159 Sky Meadow Drive
Stamford, CT 06903

Parochial/Coed
Day
Enrollment 28
Ages 6-15

Villa Maria, operated by the Roman Catholic Bernadine Franciscan Sisters, dispenses a strong dose of cod liver oil hidden in a cup of hot chocolate, to each of its 28 elementary-school-age children. The quality of education that one finds at Villa Maria, the dedication of the seven sisters and dynamo principal that make up its staff, and the bargain tuition price tag of $3,500 make this little school hard to beat.

Built in 1968 and operating since 1973 as a day school for dyslexic children, the building looks brand new. That's because the children are encouraged to develop a sense of responsibility through requiring their participation in the upkeep of the beautiful grounds and building. The staff believes that such participation helps the children to organize themselves and their time and to acquire self-discipline as well as a sense of pride. As a recent article from the magazine *Early Years* stated: "...never, ever, would the normal casualities of the struggle with learning — the pencil stubs, the art scraps, the work papers — be left abandoned in this field after the day's battle."

One parent, who could afford higher tuition elsewhere, commented: "I chose this school for its sense of serenity, for the fact that the children are polite and kind to each other and have respect for each other and the faculty." Where else do you find children standing up as a class when a visitor enters the room? "And," he added, "because real teaching takes place here."

The outstanding quality of this school is due largely to the high caliber of its teaching staff. Most have Master's degrees. The slogan "Everybody is Somebody" governs their approach to each student. While a strong academic foundation is being built, character building is occurring. It's a full-time, engrossing pursuit. Even when the nuns are not with their charges they can be found talking about them with one another as they go about their daily lives in the convent. A favorite little anecdote shows how students perceive this caring concern: one asked what the sisters did during the time they were not teaching. The sisters responded that they cooked, cleaned, corrected papers and prepared lessons. "Oh," answered the child, "then you only have fun when you're with us."

This child's observation, however, is based on outmoded concepts regarding nuns, for these are liberated women, contemporary in outlook, neat and trim in their short brown habits and veils. The principal, energetic yet soft-spoken Sister Carol Ann, is the honorary assistant coach of the New York Giants Football Team. Her active role as team promoter entitles the students to special perks like visits by the team to their school, tickets to games at the stadium, even passes into the locker room!

There is a picture-perfect, dream-like quality to the school, situated on a lush 22-acre estate once a haven for both Clare Booth Luce and writer Henry Miller. The buildings, lawns and gardens are so elegant and well-maintained that it is difficult to believe 28 children romp about them all day. The school rooms are spotless, bright and carpeted; draperies and curtains cover the windows. Two well stocked libraries, one professional and one for the students, serve the school. A large multipurpose room is used regularly as a gym and auditorium. Special labs and a plethora of neatly arranged equipment and materials such as typewriters, math machines, reading machines, tape recorders and filmstrips — much of the hardware donated, many of the materials teacher-made — are more than can ever be utilized by 28 children. Apple computers are on the way.

Reading combines linguistics and phonics. No more than four ability-grouped children are in each morning class where language, reading, spelling and math are taught. The science, social studies, fine arts, typing, special tutoring, visual and auditory perception and physical education classes are held in the afternoons and grouped according to grade level. Classes are not self-contained. The children move from room to room; each nun teaches her specialty. Monthly field trips are planned that parents help arrange and chaperone.

Many lessons are learned at Villa Maria. Perhaps the most important one is that children want and love to learn if they are in a warm, supportive environment. The hugs and kisses that accompany the students' departure in the afternoon are good indicators that at Villa Maria loving and learning go hand in hand.

SCHOOLS OF THE SOUTHEAST

BLUE RIDGE SCHOOL
Dyke, VA 22935

Private/Boys
Residential
Enrollment 225
Ages 13-19

At the foot of the Blue Ridge Mountains is a 1,000 acre campus complete with lake, swimming pool, riding trails and athletic fields. This idyllic setting, a 35-minute drive from Charlottesville, Virginia, houses Blue Ridge, a college preparatory boarding school for boys, aged 13 to 19. Founded in September 1962 on the site of a 1909 mission school, the headmaster, Hatcher Williams, saw the need for enabling boys with modest achievement test scores to develop their full potential—morally, academically, physically, and socially. Now there are 230 students and a faculty of 28, providing a 1 to 8 ratio, small classes and individual attention for each boy. The cost of attending is slightly less than $8,000 a year.

The philosophy of Blue Ridge is that the total person needs edification; if a strong moral and ethical sense is cultivated, self image, esteem and confidence will be enhanced. A boy's body and mind should be strong enough for him to contribute significantly to society; for this he needs good academic foundations and presumably higher education.

At Blue Ridge each boy starts out as a responsible, worthy person; his slate is clean. A boy can succeed in many ways and places besides the regular classroom; i.e., in sports, drama, music, art and writing. The faculty manages to make every activity a growth experience. A cross country coach gives encouragement even to the runner who finishes last. A weak writer is urged to write for the school newspaper and beams with pride when congratulated by classmates on his excellent article in print.

Academically, the students progress gradually and slowly in the ninth and tenth grades. The basics are stressed, and study and organizational skills become a part of each course. A composition is broken down into daily steps; ideas are written out, then main ideas, an outline the next day, next a rough draft and finally a completed essay. Sometimes faculty and students will tutor other students daily until they catch on. This helpful, reassuring attitude filters throughout the school.

Blue Ridge accepts potentially capable students who have either been in the wrong environment, such as a too crowded public or a too competitive private school, or those who simply need a change.

100

Blue Ridge does not advertise that it is a school for learning disabled boys. In fact, about five percent of the students would qualify for learning disabled programs, 50 percent have been labeled learning disabled in the past, and the rest probably have some specific learning difficulty. For admission the Secondary School Achievement Test, previous school records, recommendations from three teachers and two family friends and a personal interview at the school are required. Blue Ridge neither accepts boys with primary emotional or discipline problems nor the extremely gifted or handicapped. Blue Ridge wants good citizens who fall in the average range.

After admission, each student is tested to determine his abilities in basic skills. One period a day, either study skills or basic skills are taught in small groups. Otherwise, the college preparatory curriculum is taught in small classes of eight to twelve students. Teachers tutor during conference period, in the afternoon or during night study hall. A student seeks a teacher whose classroom style he likes and asks for that teacher's help. Styles and strategies run the gamut from group discovery techniques to outlining material before beginning to work. One French teacher stresses oral work but passes out an outline of each new verb tense used. Reading may involve discussion of an earlier homework assignment or reading orally and together discovering the main idea. The 28 faculty live at the school; they share and work together closely. Two faculty members have learning disability training and advise others in ways to manage problem situations.

Academics is only one part of Blue Ridge. The sports program, extensive and required every afternoon, includes football, basketball, baseball, cross-country, soccer, wrestling, track, golf, lacrosse, tennis, fencing and riding. The teams are competitive, but the coaches stress confidence and skill building. Canoeing, caving, hiking and swimming are offered as free time options. Students work on the school newspaper and yearbook, sing in the glee club, join the drama group, learn photography, create art and practice with computers. The final products of each of these groups are usually splendid, and students are justly proud of their accomplishments.

Weekends are busy and often include a trip to a nearby girl's school for a dance or party. Blue Ridge reciprocates by inviting girls to its plays, dances and sports activities.

Each student must dress neatly in a coat and tie for class, keep his room neat and be on time for classes, appointments and meals. Under the Honor System all are expected to be truthful and trustworthy. A spirit of freedom combined with individual responsibility results. Whenever a student fails to follow the rules, he receives demerits which must be worked off in the kitchen or by doing a job for the school. Serious infractions result in a discussion with the assistant headmaster, Robert Knauff, who may write the boy's parents. Next may come an executive committee hearing and possible expulsion. Drug use means automatic expulsion.

Blue Ridge seeks to develop well-rounded upright citizens. It succeeds. The students become convinced that they will be successful in life because they have experienced success at Blue Ridge.

BRANDON HALL SCHOOL
1701 Brandon Hall Dr.
Dunwoody, GA 30338

Private/Coed
Day/Residential
Enrollment 129
Ages 11-18

Once students enroll at Brandon Hall, they have little choice but to make academic progress. This 25-year-old institution did not always have a reputation for being academically demanding, but it does now. Over the past five years, enrollment has doubled and the beautifully landscaped Norman-style manor in the Dunwoody section of Atlanta, Georgia, has been further beautified. Large credit for the changes goes to present chief administrator, Colonel Harrison Kimbrell, a former Marine officer who has extensive credentials in the LD field. A primary goal of Brandon Hall is to make its students acquire the skills and knowledge necessary to function as freshmen at most four year colleges. The highly and uniquely structured college preparatory curriculum here has led to appropriate college placement for 99 percent of Brandon Hall's graduates.

Prior to admission, students must submit a creditable psycho-educational evaluation indicating they have at least normal intelligence along with a differential diagnosis showing why they are performing below their expected level. The criterion for admission does not need to be an LD diagnosis, but nearly 80 percent do have specific developmental disorders. The other 20 percent, plus many of the LD group, have experienced inconsistent previous schooling or traumatic home situations which prevented them from acquiring the study habits, skills, discipline or confidence necessary for school success. Once accepted, a student is assigned to various steps on an academic ladder. In those content courses where he is functioning at several grade levels below the norm for his age, he is placed in one-to-one tutorial classes. In other areas, he may be in a developmental class of from three to seven or in a group class of from seven to twelve. Students may move up the ladder at any time during the school year when their progress indicates they are ready for less intensive remediation and more stimulating classroom give-and-take.

At the elementary, junior high and high school levels, the 129 students may be placed in reading or language development classes before being allowed to take particular English, history, math or science courses. The fee schedule is based on the class schedule. It may be as low as $4,300 for a day student or as high as $16,000 for a boarder. Brandon Hall boards only boys; in 1983 there were 69 boarders and 60 day students of whom 42 were girls — all between the ages of 11 and 18.

Very little free time is allowed students. Usually after each class there is a 40-minute study hall where students may complete a portion of the one hour and 15 minutes of written work assigned daily for each subject. For the boarders, two hours each Saturday and Sunday are generally the maximum allowed for unsupervised activities. Throughout the weekend and on all other occasions during the week, students are under the watchful eye of the 68 teachers or proctors, 23 of whom live on campus. Proper conduct and dress are expected at all times, and 22 pages of student guidelines spell out explicitly what that conduct is to be. Teachers are expected to observe an equally strict code. All familiarity between adults and youth is according to Hoyle or Post. Boarding students must pass a rigorous room inspection at 7:30 every morning. Proper dining etiquette is ensured by a faculty member who heads each table in the dining room of the Great Hall. Meals are served family-style by student waiters. Lax or inappropriate behavior is dealt with quickly and in most instances by assigning extra work details or an additional study hall.

About 40 students graduate each year. Most enrollees are expected to complete high school at Brandon Hall, but 40 percent leave earlier. Students are not mollycoddled. Ideally, they internalize the enforced patterns of acting and thinking so that they can later cope easily with the demands of adulthood.

Few teachers at Brandon Hall are certified in learning disabilities, and there is no specialized support staff. The tendency is to hire bright liberal arts graduates and then teach them how to teach. Good adult role models are many, faculty turnover is low and many staff members have advanced degrees. Instructional supervision is handled by a headmaster and department chairpersons. Numerical grades on daily oral or written quizzes or weekly tests are submitted with the weekly reports handed in to the headmaster for each student. Parents receive copies of the written six-week cumulative reports. Upon the completion of each course, including some advanced placement courses, standardized tests are given.

Physical education is offered daily. Students also may take classes in art, music, journalism, drama and speech. There is not currently the space, equipment or time for other curricular offerings such as computer courses, but a major development program is underway to alleviate the crowded conditions and to enhance the program. Planned weekend outings are of unusually high caliber.

Anticipated over the next decade is the addition of a modern gymnasium which will house additional classrooms, offices, labs and recreational space. Parents are not expected to underwrite the funding for the projected growth, but support for the program seems high. Additional dorms will probably be built to alleviate the cramped conditions in the two dormitories. Tutorials are currently given in the students' bedrooms. The dynamic growth of the school in recent years suggests this phased expansion will come to pass, but the conservative philosophy of the school and the gracious ambience of the 30-acre manorial setting will likely remain.

Educational jargon is taboo at Brandon Hall. Students can't use their handicap as an excuse for failure. They are expected to produce and perform despite any disability. From the outset, teachers are made aware of students' weaknesses and strengths, but the assumption is that hard work and rigidly consistent adherence to prescribed modes of instruction and control will enable a student to catch up and stay caught up. One student claimed she had learned more Latin in her first class session at Brandon Hall than she had in two years at her previous school. Comparably bold attestations to academic progress are generally the rule at Brandon Hall. Doubters and detractors need only reflect on how efficiently they managed to learn when isolated over long periods of time with adult authority figures.

THE CENTER SCHOOL
3200 Woodbine St.
Chevy Chase, MD 20815

Private/Coed
Day
Enrollment 90
Ages 6-14

A typical brick school building set against a wooded slope overlooks Rock Creek Park in Montgomery County, Maryland. In 1980, this former public school was converted by Dr. Rugh Spodak into a private day school for LD students of average to high intelligence without primary emotional problems.

The 30 full-time and 5 part-time Center staff members work either in small groups or individually with eight or fewer students at a time. A daily one-to-one tutorial taught by an academic therapist trained in the Orton-Gillingham method is scheduled for each child. An art teacher, two physical education teachers, a language-speech pathologist, a psychologist and three administrators complement the teaching staff.

The school takes pains to admit only those students who are felt to be capable of returning in two or three years to nonspecialized schools.

Most are mildly to moderately LD. A small portion is gifted; these students tend to have severe learning problems. It's too early to know how good the school's predictions are since the school has been in existence but a few years, but thus far only one of the 14 who have left has required placement in a special education program. Although the psychological testing that precedes admission may consist of only a WISC-R and Bender, the day long visit to the school allows enough time to assess informally the child's level of intellectual functioning. After previous school and testing records are reviewed and admission has been granted, a full battery of diagnostic tests are given so as to design appropriate programs and to place children correctly at their developmental levels. The school places considerable emphasis on writing; several of the tests administered include structured and unstructured writing samples, as well as near and far point copying.

In order to help students develop necessary academic skills, instructors break almost all tasks down into sequential learning steps. At the beginning of each class an oral and written schedule of activities is presented. The specific skill on which an individual or small group is ;working is then broken down; the steps are written on paper, a chart or the blackboard. In English class oral expression is taught by the teacher presenting material in a clear, simple, organized manner at the student's language level. The students are then taught to organize their thoughts and to present them aloud. As soon as a student is capable, he moves to written expression. Record keeping and journal writing are weekly activities; every child has a notebook. Elementary reading skills are taught by the Orton-Gillingham-trained tutors. The more advanced students learn study skills and work on abstract reading concepts. A highly structured and sequential approach is also used in the individual or small group math sessions.

In art class planned projects are likewise presented as a series of progressive tasks. Students must first follow and copy the teacher's example; "Cut here, fold there." They are then allowed more freedom to create and develop their own ideas. The initial projects are always finished by the end of the period so that the child has the satisfaction of taking it home the same day.

Physical education emphasizes basic ball skills and body movement. Soccer, basketball and softball are the three major sports. The children learn one skill at a time, i.e., how to kick, run, catch or throw. In soccer, for example, a whole period may be spent learning how to head the ball; first the child practices on his own, then with a partner and finally in a modified game. Regulation games are played when the prerequisite skills have been mastered.

The Center School program for the gifted seeks to stretch the students intellectually while giving appropriate remedial instruction. An enriched curriculum is provided in science and social studies. A trained anthropologist conducts these classes and serves as a resource staff person for the other teachers. Physics and algebra are taught to some of the older students. In an intermediate level science class the shape and movements of the solar system were described and discussed using the correct technical terminology.

Center believes in giving praise and rewards for academic successes. The development of a positive self-concept and social coping skills are considered as important as school progress, however. The director and the staff psychologist meet the students individually to become acquainted and discuss problems. Twice-weekly parent discussion groups take place during which parents share problems and successes.

Discipline is individually handled by the teacher, but generally the student is shown how to behave and is then praised whenever he acts accordingly. Repeated misbehavior might lead to a discussion with the psychologist in order to uncover the child's feelings and the real source of the problem. In extreme cases suspension may be necessary. Parent involvement is mandatory; at least once a month parents must attend a meeting at the school. However, many become quite active as classroom aides or group discussion participants.

The Center School physical plant is a one-floor building. Six large classrooms are partitioned so that twelve groups of eight each may meet simultaneously. Noise carries from one room to the next, but the sound is low enough not to distract. The library is partitioned into numerous small cubbyholes in which a teacher and a student or two may have a tutorial. An art room, a supply room, offices and a gymnasium large enough for basketball occupy the rest of the ground floor. On the basement level is a preschool, a testing center and a community tutoring service. Three terraced, blacktopped playgrounds and two playing fields are available for outdoor recreation.

Tuition at Center is $7,700; a few students are funded, and several receive scholarship assistance. The youngsters wear uniforms and are generally neat in appearance. All provide their own transportation.

The Center School provides an excellent, ordered learning environment for its 90 boys and girls. The combination of individual tutoring, curricular structure, small classes, parental involvement and sequential progress seems to work very effectively. One parent who thought her child would never read declared the boy now chose to spend his free time with books, a feat she called miraculous.

CRESTWOOD HALL
941 S. New Hope Rd.
Gastonia, NC 28052

Private/Coed
Day
Enrollment 25
Ages 6-15

In 1973, parents of 39 dyslexic children in Gastonia, North Carolina, began urging local school authorities to provide specially trained teachers and state-funded remediation programs for their learning handicapped youngsters. These rather distraught but determined parents little expected that some of them would soon become school authorities and administrators themselves. But the outcome of their ten-year-long saga of grass roots research, journalistic controversy and court litigation was the establishment of a private, not-for-profit day school that they ran themselves.

In searching for a viable alternative to the existing programs for dyslexics, the group became acquainted with and intrigued by the work of Dr. Charles Shedd. Shortly before Shedd died, he urged the Gastonia vanguard to start its own school, and he supplied them with a conceptual framework with which to begin. Individual community contributions led to the establishment of the Dyslexia School of North Carolina in a vacated orthopedic center, alongside a series of handsome social service agency facilities on Gaston County property. The name was later changed to Crestwood Hall, and the program was disassociated from the network of Shedd-sponsored schools. Dr. Patricia Hardman, who had adopted the Shedd ideas and techniques for several schools around the country, took on an important advisory role.

The Hardman rationale includes the following premises: (1) the developmental dyslexic and the hyperkinetic child profit from the use of extremely organized instructional materials in the fields of math, reading and grammar which introduce only one new variable at a time; (2) the child needs to progress from the concrete level of learning in which "hands on" materials and multisensory activities as well as rote drill are emphasized to the functional-manipulative level and then finally to the abstract level; (3) the child must learn to extract information according to the techniques learned earlier, i.e., when using general science and social studies texts; (4) reading must emphasize comprehension after completion of each phonetically-structured linguistic instructional segment; (5) complete mastery and constant success are imperative; (6) the child must recognize the natural consequences of his actions and the desirability of postponing need gratification; (7) proper diet and consistently firm home management are invaluable in treating and remediating the students accepted into a program organized along Hardman lines. The fully LD-certified staff of six teachers totally ascribes to the Hardman philosophy.

A typical day at Crestwood incorporates all of the Hardman

principles. There is a minimum of extraneous conversation. All children are addressed as Mister or Miss, and they are expected to react appropriately throughout the school day to simple cues such as "Books, please," "Let's begin" or "Page 45.". The routine is such that improper work or behavior is mainly handled by assigning a student to Station Two, an area for brief after-school detentions, or by turning a child's desk to the outside of the classroom. During instruction time, a class will respond to a teacher's question or statement with a simultaneous, robot-like and most vociferous repetition of a previously learned fact, definition or word spelling. These loud, resonant replies somewhat resemble pentecostal litanies or the spectator responses to cheerleaders. They purportedly serve to stimulate the auditory and oral modality channels, as well as to reinforce the learning of crucial information. The time spent on reading and composition is not so orchestrated, but the classes in history, science and social values incorporate a comparable pedagogical technique. Shedd-inspired or oriented materials are used almost exclusively. The daily period for physical education is spent on sequential tasks designed to increase the child's sense of laterality, time and spatial awareness, and synchronized movement.

Even at lunchtime, the children seem mindful of and yet relaxed about the superimposed and extremely structured routine, which extends to the kind and quantity of food brought from home. Each child's lunch is a high-protein, low-carbohydrate meal containing neither processed foods, milk, cola or citric acid. Few, if any, products contain refined sugar or starch. The Crestwood staff holds to the view that dyslexia and hyperkinesis are in part caused by food allergies or metabolic imbalances and that both these conditions can be alleviated by proper diet. Many students are on vitamin therapy; none are permitted to be on behavior-control drugs.

So far, no one has determined which are the critical variables that account for Crestwood's success in bringing about academic remediation and good social adjustment. But on-site observation of the 125 enrolled elementary-school-age students and review of the follow-up study done on former students attest to how well matched the Crestwood regimen and its student body are. Within two years, most Crestwood students return to a regular elementary classroom where they function at their chronological grade level without additional remedial work. Standardized tests (the CTBS and the Gray oral untimed SAT) are given three times a year and serve as the measure of readiness to go back to a conventional school program. The staff are quick to note that continued success is dependent upon the degree to which their students internalize the learning procedures they are taught.

The parents, during the preliminary testing and evaluation of their child, agree in advance that they will pay the $2,300 tuition on schedule, that they will change their lives around to accommodate the developmental needs of their particular child and the program emphases at Crestwood, and that when problems arise they will consult directly with the school staff. Some parents drive 50-mile distances four times daily in order to abide by the Crestwood credo. This intense degree of cooperation between home and school may ultimately turn out to be the crucial difference that makes the Crestwood program work.

DAVISON SCHOOL
1500 N. Decatur NE
Atlanta, GA 30306

Private/Coed
Day
Enrollment 52
Ages 3-18

The Davison School, Inc., was founded in 1928 by Mrs. Louise Davison for the express purpose of teaching speech and language to children whose communicative ability was severely impaired. Through the years, it has carried out this mission splendidly. The school, located in the Druid Hills residential section of Atlanta, Georgia, near Emory University, is housed in an attractive, old mansion. Four children occupy each of the house's large, well-kept bedrooms; classrooms and administrative additions are in a pleasant, pine-paneled newer wing.

Davison has 52 students, 35 of whom are boarders; students' ages range from 3 to 18. All students attend for an 11-month year. They go to camp together for one week in July, at which time newcomers get acquainted and self-help skills are emphasized.

Davison is fully accredited by the American Speech-Language-Hearing Association and depends on its $5,300 tuition and its $6,700 boarding fee to cover its operational costs. Often, because of the speech and language therapy, a portion of the family's expense is covered by insurance.

Before admission, each student is carefully and individually evaluated by a team of two speech pathologists who consult with the director, Dr. Lucille Pressnell, and, if necessary, a psychologist. A battery of speech, language, hearing and achievement tests is given. The child is also observed in the school setting. Dr. Pressnell looks for discrepancy patterns between the child's verbal and performance testing in order to ascertain whether the child would profit from and fit into the program. All students have a moderate to severe speech or language problem, many are multihandicapped or aphasic and some have below average intelligence. The potential for language learning is the criterion for acceptance. A child whose emotional immaturity and behavior are deemed to be potentially disruptive of the school's disciplined routine is not accepted.

Each September, standardized achievement tests are given, and students are screened anew for vision and hearing. Approximately seven students are assigned to each class; placement is based on the student's age, achievement level, language functioning, need for individual attention and ability to work with others. The staff feels its students need total immersion in language therapy. Each student receives daily individual speech and language therapy or learning disability tutoring.

Useful social and linguistic skills are stressed in all academic and social areas. For example, when students receive letters from home, resident staff help children to answer the questions orally and then they are taught to write out these replies and thus correspond. Even in math classes, which might consist of a trip to a grocery store to buy snacks, communication is stressed. In history, texts are read aloud and then discussed. Teachers eat with their students and encourage the development of good language, polite behavior and positive social relationships. The dormitory houseparents take time to listen and to improve language skills. This warm, supportive atmosphere considerably hastens linguistic self-confidence. So successful is this approach that one 12-year-old who began the year uttering only a few words was using short sentences within six months.

Speech and language are taught using an analytical, phonetic method developed by Mrs. Davison. The child learns to recognize each sound when he hears and sees it, then to say and write it. This approach incorporates the visual, auditory and kinesthetic modalities and is especially effective with aphasic children. Once a sound is learned, it is combined with others to form words. The approach is highly structured, formal and consistent. Within a group, children are regimented. Even kindergarteners must wait politely for their turn to speak.

The staff has been headed by Dr. Pressnell since 1972. It consists of four speech pathologists, eight special education teachers, a recreation therapist, an occupational therapist, a consulting psychologist and seven houseparents. The whole staff interacts so warmly with the student body that Davison appears to be an extension of a large, happy family. Parents are encouraged to contact the staff at any time. They are especially urged to attend the special programs presented five times a year by the parents' association. Quarterly written reports are sent to the home.

Basic skills are emphasized in the physical education program, just as they are in the academic classes. A Davison student will typically have more than one handicap, each of which will receive attention. The physical therapist and occupational therapist work individually with those who have problems with motor coordination or sensory integration. After school and on weekends, a variety of recreational activities is planned by the physical education and arts and crafts instructors to reinforce the training of the special therapists. The boarders take part in frequent recreational and cultural events within the greater Atlanta community. Students at Emory volunteer as scout leaders, Big Sisters and pen pals.

A student's communicative ability is the major determinant of readiness to leave Davison. The children who are of kindergarten age may stay only one year and then be ready for mainstreaming. But others, the more severely impaired who enter at a later age, often stay until they are 18. Some are mainstreamed and then go on to college. Two former students are presently at Piedmont College. Others are advised to develop vocational skills. The widely divergent ability levels of Davison students are matched by a commensurate school commitment to counsel all students realistically regarding their future. Davison's overriding purpose and goals are to enable each student to reach his maximum potential. Davison can be proud of its success in this undertaking.

THE DEVELOPMENTAL CENTER ACADEMY
7823 Mushinski Rd.
Tampa, FL 33624

Private/Coed
Day/Residential
Enrollment 61
Ages 6-18

An intriguing and ambitious experiment has been going on at the Center Academy of Tampa, Florida. It's not a short-lived, trial-and-error sort of thing. Rather, it is an instructional undertaking that is both humanistic and scientific. The Academy, like its two counterparts elsewhere, is an extension of the clinical services and philosophical orientation of the Developmental Center, a 16-year-old neuropsychological institute in St. Petersburg, Florida. The academies came into being soon after Dr. Mack R. Hicks, the Center's founder-director, realized that many of his youthful clients had school problems that began when it was assumed they were ready to read. He realized what they might really need was one-to-one reading help.

Although each Academy could be called a school, the Center avoids use of this label, preferring instead to describe the three academies as "full day intensive treatment programs for children" who have normal (or above average) intelligence and "demonstrate maturational problems such as learning disabilities, dyslexia, hyperactivity, disorganization, writing problems, coordination problems, low self-esteem, low frustration tolerance and low motivation." The recommended length of stay is usually three semesters and one summer. One nonboarding Academy program is located in Pinellas Park, Florida; another is in London, England; the third is the day and residential school-like program at El Ranchero in northwestern Tampa.

El Ranchero is a 20-acre ranch. Moss-draped trees, a tall barn-type structure and an elongated building painted to resemble the facade of an Old West town dominate the center of the campus. A huge spring-fed swimming pool, groups of children riding horseback and a flood-ravaged ravine add to the impression that this is truly a ranch. But there are no farmhands and no livestock other than the horses boarded at a nearby stable. The ranch setting has been adopted because it is believed to contribute to feelings of wholesomeness and relaxation and to stimulate the imaginations of the 61 boys and girls at this Academy.

The children range in age from 6 to 18. Some travel daily to and from homes 50 miles away. A dozen children reside on campus with the Center Family in two homelike dormitories managed by resident staff. The cost of a year's tuition is $4,000; for boarders, $12,000. Students are initially tested and evaluated by certified, licensed clinical psychologists at the Developmental Center. Of the thousand or more clients of the Center each year, very few are recommended for placement at the Academies. When they are recommended, parents are sometimes able, with the help of the Center, to obtain third-party insurance reimbursement for their child's academic therapy. Two of the Center's future goals are to have the residential program accredited as an out-patient facility and to have the Academy actually become a working ranch. Another immediate goal is to have the Academy approved for issuance of a GED high school equivalency certificate.

Students at the Academy seem to be happy, polite and industrious. Currently, they have the option of being paid a dollar or so for 30 minutes' worth of maintenance work. The Center believes that children need to develop a strong sense of self along with a respect for traditional values, i.e., the work ethic.

In the academic areas the name of the game is "catch up." A structured remedial program designed for each child utilizes many different reading materials, including VAAD, a visual reading program developed by the Center director. Each program is geared to basic skill acquisition and individual ego building; new foundations are built on existing ones. Children may proceed on their own from page to page and unit to unit if the written papers they regularly submit receive a "grade" of at least 80 percent. No more than 15 children are in each class, overseen in each instance by one "clinician" (or teacher) and an aide. The aide's responsibility essentially is to grade the children's papers. If a child's work is not 80 percent correct, the child is summoned to the teacher's desk and the two work together until any errors and confusion are eliminated.

Besides the five clinicians and four aides at the Academy, there are several resident staff persons; a person in charge of the sophisticated educational hardware; and two administrators, one of whom directs the Pinellas Park Academy as well. None of the clinicians are certified in LD; they are college graduates who receive on-the-job training and instructions from the Academy Director, the psychometricians on the Center staff, a curriculum specialist and Dr. Hicks. The director meets weekly with the clinicians and reviews each child's progress and treatment program.

From the time a child is first placed at the Academy, the parents know what they can reasonably expect from the program. Written evaluations and parent conferences occur quarterly. In addition, the projections for each child are upgraded yearly and include a tentative timetable for referring a child out (or placement elsewhere) along with possible specific schools. An on-going relationship usually continues with someone from the Center until no further help or treatment is needed in the new school setting. All 85 of the Center's personnel are available as resources to the Academy, even though each facility is expected to be a self-supporting unit.

The Center is determined to have a positive impact on the well-being of the communities it serves, and in this regard it has begun a Saturday program for needy, developmentally disabled youngsters, called S.O.S. In soliciting funds to help cover the S.O.S. expenses, the Center claims it has been successful in solving children's problems because it has been "unhindered by labeling requirements, red tape, quotas or diagnostic formulas." By issuing to interested subscribers a highly literate series of publications titled *Parent, Child and Community*, the rather fundamental Center philosophy and advice are shared with a wide audience.

To measure the Center's effectiveness, in 1983, a random poll was taken with a mailed questionnaire. Of the 264 replies received, 19 percent had attended the Academy. The others had either been evaluated at the Center, received one-to-one remediation or had psychotherapy there, attended the summer program or had been adult family members receiving therapy. The changes reported in the status of problems since treatment appeared significant, especially in the areas of listening, writing skills, concentration and motivation. Rankings of good, excellent or outstanding were given to 95 percent of the diagnostic and treatment programs provided the respondents.

The Center and the Academies are obviously serving a need. The clinical therapy model is both new-fangled and old-fashioned; the teachers are clinicians. It remains to be seen whether this distinctive approach to the remediation of learning disabilities has permanent merit. The chances are that enough research will be conducted by the Center in the future both to modify and verify the developments it seeks to direct.

THE LAB SCHOOL OF WASHINGTON, D.C.
4759 Reservoir Rd., N.W.
Washington, D.C. 20007

Private/Coed
Day
Enrollment 125
Ages 5-16

In the nation's capital, thanks to an innovative approach to learning, more than 200 moderately to severely learning disabled youngsters have gained access to the world of organized thought and resourceful productivity which they might otherwise never have entered. Sally L. Smith perceived from working with her own LD son that the universal language of the arts could be the key whereby learning-impaired children might acquire the inner perception, organization and discrimination they needed to function in and make sense of the cosmos around them. She assembled and has directed over the past 17 years a uniquely talented staff in order that her ideas might be implemented. Her experimental day school began as an offshoot of the diagnostic and tutorial services of the Kingsbury Center.

In September, 1983, the Lab School changed its location from its crowded Phelps Place address and Kingsbury Center affiliation to a new base near the foreign embassies and city reservoir. The large brownstone and brick facility it now occupies accommodates 125 boys and girls, aged 5 to 16. The tuition is $7,800 for the lower school and $200 extra for the upper school. During 1982-1983, the District of Columbia paid full tuition for 50 students; six students from Virginia and Maryland were also tuition-reimbursed. In the past the socioeconomic backgrounds of the Lab School student body have been quite diverse; 25 percent, for instance, were black. All have had in common a normal to above average intelligence, a serious learning disability and no primary emotional disturbance.

The nongraded academic program of the Lab School contains both an open and a hidden agenda. Implicit in all instruction is the underlying belief that the developmental needs of its students can be met through incorporation of artistic principles both in "standard" remedial classes and in the "extras." Ingenious curricular materials, techniques and strategies are used throughout the day to motivate students, to challenge their imaginations and to hasten their intellectual maturity.

At the elementry level, half of each day is spent in individualized diagnostic teaching of reading, writing, spelling, arithmetic and perceptual skills. For the rest of the day, students are immersed in art, woodwork, graphic arts, music, dance, drama, film-making or *Academic Clubs*. The clubs are an engrossing, multisensory means of teaching the social sciences and reading readiness through active, vivid and concrete involvement with the cultural lore of various historical eras from caveman days to the present. During club-time, an artist presents history in such a way that students seem to live it. In the Immigrants' Club, while hearing tales of early settlers' everyday lives, children prepare foods the way settlers did and create furnished models of their houses. Members of the Renaissance Club act the parts of famous people, such as Leonardo da Vinci and Lorenzo de Medici, and help to paint a mural of Florence, complete with perspective, while listening to a story of a boy living in the late 1500s. During the afternoon, children also hear great literature read aloud, conduct scientific experiments and take part in physical education activities that emphasize gross motor skill development, eye-hand coordination, direction following and timing.

At the junior high level, similar goals and pursuits exist, but academics and independent study are stressed. Within small groups, students are taught how to address a task and which sequential steps to take; they then work on their own with the teacher checking often to reinforce progress or correct errors. Each morning after assembly, students have four 45-minute periods; one in math; another in a tutorial for reading, spelling and/or study skills; and two classes in either science, American history, U.S. geography, language arts (written and expressive) or business and life skills. The last course operates like an Academic Club, only here students become involved in a commercial enterprise and learn how to form a corporation, to produce and sell a product, to use the telephone book, to advertise, to budget, to fill out forms and to keep records. About five times a year, the junior high students *open* a restaurant. This traditionally gourmet endeavor incorporates all the arts, plus history, geography, social skills and math. One and a half hours daily are spent in an arts elective or a course such as typing, sex or driver education. The afternoon sports program includes swimming, gymnastics and ball games and emphasizes acquiring the fitness and skills necessary for fun sports participation.

The Lab School's library is really a media center filled with "talking books." Each lower school student comes there every day to listen to taped or recorded literary works. Junior high students needing an auditory presentation come for two to five periods a week and may read along with the recording or not. At the end of each chapter, the student discusses characters, setting, plot and meaning with the media specialist and then proceeds independently to a new chapter.

Local artists at the Lab School outnumber the regular full-time staff of 11 classroom teachers, each of the latter of whom has a Master's degree and certification in LD. The enthusiastic and skilled artists, who serve part-time, bring freshness to the curriculum, relief to the teachers, and inestimable rewards to students. Most LD students have highly sensitive antennae and pick up quickly on the wordless symbols of art. Through woodworking, graphic arts and film, children develop visual motor skills and reading readiness. Music heightens auditory perception. Dance provides sensory motor training by enabling a child to organize his body movement in space. A dance teacher discovered four students could not move backwards; after acquiring this ability, their skill to subtract and use the past tense improved. Puppetry and drama present opportunities to sort and classify affective cues associated, for instance, with the behavior of a strong king or a shy person, as well as to improve speech and language. Bart, aged 9, first learned to associate sounds with symbols by beating a drum when a red chip was held up or tapping it when a yellow chip was presented. From there, he went on to associate sounds with letter symbols. Raymond, aged 12, learned to focus on visual details in film making and to put sequential scenes in order.

Besides the full-time teachers and the artists who direct the clubs and arts activities, there are always interns from American University. Many of these have had years of teaching experience but are finishing a degree in LD instruction. Sally Smith, the Lab School's founder-director, is also the professor in charge of the LD Program of the College of Education of American University. Besides providing an intensive, quality remedial education for her Lab School students, Mrs. Smith wishes to continue to pioneer in new methods and techniques, to train teachers and to disseminate the Lab School programs. Helping the administration, teachers, artists and interns are a consulting clinical psychologist, an occupational therapist, a speech pathologist-language therapist and the media center specialists. All work as a team, sharing and advising regularly on individual or general academic questions.

The Lab School schedules several field trips for its students. Each fits carefully into prescribed classroom goals. Beforehand, each student studies background information and forms a good picture of what he expects to see. Afterwards, by writing an outline or a paper, drawing a picture, or in some other way tying the experience into a meaningful whole, students are helped to remember and organize what they saw.

The integration of disorganized fragments into a comprehensive pattern is the Lab School's overall goal, Preadmission testing, placement screening, periodic reviews of progress and formal standardized testing each May comprise the testing program.

Parent counseling, twice-annual parent conferences and a 12-page narrative report in June all exist to inform parents and staff on how a student is developing. Typically, because standardized tests often do not measure affective changes nor improvement in basic perceptual organization, significant academic gains do not show up until a year and a half goes by. After age 11, extraordinary progress is often recorded — three to six years in a year. Much of this progress can be attributed to the neural maturation that can occur at puberty and to the systematically taught and programmed learning through the arts. Students in the lower school usually stay five years; junior high students tend to stay three. Upon their returning to a regular school placement, tutoring is frequently recommended. Students dislike leaving the Lab School, but they have proven successful in traditional schools, and a number of them are now doing well in college.

LD educators and parents would be wise to explore the premises and practices advocated by Sally Smith. A slide-tape show and teaching films produced at the school have been shown nationwide. Sally Smith's *No Easy Answers, The Learning Disabled Child at Home and at School* (Bantam Edition/1981) is a valuable compendium of the Lab School philosophy. All in all, the innovative programs of this remarkable school are worthy of emulation nationwide by teachers of all kinds of students, but especially the learning disabled.

MORNING STAR SCHOOL   *Diocesan/Coed*
210 E. Linebaugh   *Day*
Tampa, FL 33612   *Enrollment 72*
                                                        Ages 6-16

Even on hot or humid days it's refreshing to be at the Morning Star School in Tampa, Florida. The students are happy. They work hard. They love their teachers. This climate is attributable to top class administrative acumen, for the history of this Morning Star School (there are three others in the state) is one of adapting to changing community needs to the extent of thrice changing the kind of students served. But the school holds steadfastly to a fundamental philosophy, that of Vatican II. Begun in 1958 through the efforts of a Catholic Archbishop to give physically handicapped youth a chance to reach their full intellectual, social and moral capabilities, it now serves 72 elementary and junior high boys and girls of average intelligence who were unable to function in a regular school setting. Despite a wide diversity in the backgrounds of the student body, all seem to have acquired a remarkably similar degree of motivation and set of values.

Like its affiliates, this Morning Star operates under the auspices of the Catholic diocese, adjoins the grounds of a parochial school and offers religious guidance, albeit of a nonsectarian nature. It has otherwise developed quite independently of the church. Ms. Jeanette Friedheim, the school's guiding star, left the sisterhood of St. Joseph at about the same time that this order relinquished its role in managing and staffing the school. All staff are lay persons now and are certified special educators.

From the start, curricular emphases had been in the areas of motor and language development. This program expertise was well suited to the new curriculum for learning disabled. Because of Morning Star's reputation for having an outstanding program in perceptual development and adaptive physical education, a high proportion of the students come needing help with body coordination. Mrs. Mary Twachtman, who conducts this program, is such a powerhouse that her pupils regularly win Special Physical Fitness and CHAMP awards. This same teacher also conducts weekly group therapy sessions, and, by popular demand, she teaches the sex education unit of the health classes.

Language arts are taught daily, and strong emphasis is placed on receptive and expressive language skills. As with reading and math, skills are mastered through individualized and small group instruction using a variety of simple but clever materials and a systematic check list process. Whenever a child fails to succeed, the specific learning task is reanalyzed and new approaches are tried. Subject matter content at the upper levels is mainly taught through reading and discussion. Each Friday teachers hand in lesson plans for the following week so that the principal may evaluate them and make any necessary changes.

Inherent in the Morning Star philosophy is the assumption that parents will play an active role in ensuring the child's continuing progress. Twice-annual parent conferences, quarterly report cards, bimonthly meetings of the Parents' Auxiliary and mandatory participation by families in the up-keep and fundraising activities of the school foster a close rapport between students, staff and parents. Since the $1,250 regular tuition represents but 40 percent of the per-pupil cost, money is raised through the efforts of the parents' association, the rest coming through diocesan subsidy or donations. Involvement by community volunteers and personnel from neighboring universities in providing screening or instructional assistance is extensive and effective.

As part of this low cost school program, besides advising the staff on educational matters, the school's consulting psychologist works with parents in prescribing constructive ways of managing problems that might develop with their children in the home.

The facilities and instructional materials at Morning Star are adequate and appropriate for the age levels served. Resourceful use is made of numerous simple recreational materials in the accomplishment of educational objectives. Students use the library and sports facilities of the adjacent parochial school; they also eat lunch there, and the older students are mainstreamed into some of the regular classes. Uniforms are worn by the younger children so that they will not appear different from their parochial school counterparts. Each year, the Morning Star student body takes part in an Ecology Day during which the building and grounds are spruced up. The campus tends to remain well kept in the interval, and classrooms stay orderly and attractive. The overall impression is that the children enjoy what they're doing, who they are and where they are.

Admission requirements involve the provision of a psychological evaluation and evidence of an IQ of at least 80. Achievement levels are determined by staff-administered tests, and, from these records, existing spaces in the various ability-based class levels are then filled. Salaries of the nine faculty members, all of whom have LD or special education certification, are close to those paid in the public schools, and rapport with and support from the principal are such that turnover of staff is no problem. Most children stay from two to five years, after which they return to a regular public or parochial school.

Morning Star's concern has always been that a positive self-concept is necessary before a child can function happily in society. Although pitfalls will confront Morning Star's children in subsequent schooling and life, the headstart they receive in the wholesome, nonthreatening Morning Star environment tends to assure a successful future.

OAKWOOD SCHOOL
7210 Braddock Rd.
Annandale, VA 22003

Private/Coed
Day
Enrollment 90
Ages 5-16

A spacious brick colonial building in a northern Virginia residential area, conveniently located a few minutes drive from Interstate 495, houses Oakwood School. This alternative coeducational day school serves learning disabled students, aged 5 to 16, who need small classes rather than just resource room help; their disabilities are not so severe that a self-contained LD class in a public school would be recommended. Formerly known as the Children's Achievement Center, the Oakwood School was founded by Director Bob McIntyre with one student in 1971. It now has 90 students, a staff of 12 special education teachers, two psychologists, two adaptive physical educational specialists, an occupational therapist, three speech therapists and three academic supervisors.

Bob McIntyre likens his school to a mission house that provides caring support and a holistic, respectful instructional regimen to those it serves. Although there are no religious services, the Judeo-Christian view of man permeates the school. Teachers display loving concern, and the students respond with spontaneous courtesy and healthy self-esteem. Discipline is nonpunitive. Redirection and positive reinforcement occur first. Giving "sticker" rewards or granting students the treasured privilege of private recreation time serves to motivate youngsters to develop good social skills. If problems need a more direct approach, a disruptive student may be moved into an alcove of the classroom or he/she may talk through the problem with the psychologist. The childrens' relaxed, happy countenances give evidence of the system's viability.

For admission, Oakwood requires a full psychoeducational battery of tests and an evaluation of speech and language. Even if testing has been done elsewhere, Oakwood requires a personal interview and some short form of testing at the school. Students are accepted who have low average or above IQ or who give evidence of more potential even if the IQ is in the 70s. Behavior must be considered manageable, and a learning disability must be the primary problem. Depending on the individual program, the tuition may be between $4,700 and $6,730 per year.

At the beginning of the school year, each child receives diagnostic testing to determine class placement and special learning needs. At this time, a full speech, language and hearing evaluation is done, as is an evaluation by the adaptive physical education specialist.

Oakwood keeps its parents informed about progress. Every Friday during the school year, a folder goes home to show parents work samples. Teachers often call parents more than once a month to report on progress. Twice a year, school is closed for a few days for conferences.

Class size ranges from five to 12 students with one teacher. Class groupings are made according to age, grade level and ability. Two hours each day the students are regrouped for reading and math according to skill level. Each student's program is individualized, but one-to-one individualization only occasionally occurs. Small group work is stressed so that students will be better prepared to function in the mainstream later.

Acquisition of basic skills in reading and math get top priority. Among other distinctive program features is the "social-affective"curriculum under the supervision of the school psychologist which is integrated into every program. Basal readers and standard math texts are used to provide a traditional approach. Remedial strategies may be brought in to strengthen weak modalities. Oakwood's students often succeed without remedial or compensatory help, but the educational supervisors program extra help if necessary. Adaptive physical education concentrates on throwing, catching, kicking and body movement within innovative game situations. The students all learn group sports, but skills rather than winning are emphasized. Some students with particular motor problems work individually with the instructor. Speech and language programs are top notch, for the class with the youngest students is taught by a speech-language pathologist, and one half of the student body receives individual therapy two to three times weekly. Sensory training is provided by an occupational therapist for a few students one day a week.

Oakwood is comfortably housed in a single building. The therapy rooms and classrooms are spacious and full of light. A multipurpose room used for indoor physical education and recess and periodic drama club productions has a weight room adjoining. Art is taught within the classroom by the regular teacher; music appreciation is provided by the media specialist. Elementary science laboratory kits are used in the classrooms for lack of a lab. Students bring their own lunch and eat in a lunchroom. Outside, there is space for basketball, soccer and baseball.

Bob McIntyre's goal is to instill within his students feelings of self-respect and dignity. Oakwood's setting seems to build youthful self-confidence no matter where a student is functioning academically. Within the small supportive classrooms, its students thrive socially and emotionally. Concern for the whole child — spiritually, physically and mentally — is Oakwood's strength.

THE PATTERSON SCHOOL
Rt. 5 Box 170
Lenoir, NC 28645

Private/Coed
Day/Residential
Enrollment 114
Ages 12-19

Few settings can match the pastoral beauty of the Patterson School's mountainside campus. There, several miles northeast of Lenoir, North Carolina, a cluster of old and modern Georgian-style buildings overlooks playing fields, woodlands and the Yadkin River Valley. In 1909, this 1,400-acre site was donated to the Episcopal Church so that it might establish a traditional college preparatory school. Alumni have been returning ever since to enjoy the Patterson landscape and to reassure themselves that things have not changed too much.

Three times in the last decade the old grads have had to chastize the administration: once for overemphasizing athletic competition, once for overspending and once for being lax regarding student discipline and conduct. One significant change occurred five years ago, however, that initially escaped the notice of the Old Guard. This occurred when the Board agreed to implement a suggestion of the school's consulting psychologist, who happened also to operate a summer camp for dyslexics on the Patterson School grounds. The suggestion was to accept learning disabled students and to provide a special supplementary program for them during the regular school year. The Board agreed to implement the program on the condition that no more than 30 LD students be enrolled at any one time. The arrangement has worked out well for all concerned, and each year the waiting list to get into the program grows longer, even though it costs $1,500 over and above the $5,890 rate for annual tuition, room and board.

121

Several features of the Patterson program make it well suited to LD students. Of primary importance are the services of two language therapists. Each meets five days a week for 50 minutes daily with two students at a time. An Orton-Gillingham type, multisensory, phonetic approach is used, and, depending on the student's area of weakness, different specific skill mastery materials are employed. The psycho-educational evaluation required of all students before admission into the program must have shown that the student had at least an IQ of 105, was dyslexic and was no more than two years below grade level in any basic skill area. Pretesting and posttesting occur frequently in order to measure progress and to ascertain the value of and need for more diagnostic work.

All students must be able to keep pace with the regular college preparatory curriculum. At least 16 academic units are required for graduation, of which four must be in English, three in math, and two each in science, social studies and foreign language. Intervention occurs quickly and frequently whenever a student's work begins to slip. All Patterson students are expected to avail themselves of the opportunity to work with a tutor each afternoon; anyone who has a D grade or below must have tutoring until that grade improves. Almost all of the 21 staff members live on campus, and they interact on many different levels with the 125 students, so that an informal counseling relationship is always in effect. Five evenings a week there is supervised study. Those who have above a 2.0 average may study in their rooms for the hour and a half; the others must study in the dining hall. Every three weeks, printed interim reports are sent to parents which describe their child's academic performance, behavior, attitude and interest in each subject matter area. When these reports indicate a student is doing unsatisfactory work, the pupil is placed on academic probation and denied the right to leave campus. Rule infractions require their nullification by Sunday afternoon detention or Saturday afternoon work periods of 30 minutes each.

Classes are small, and the quality of instruction is commendable. In spite of the emphasis on academics, a modicum of leniency is granted the LD student in that in certain classes tape recorders or calculators may be used and tests may be administered separately or orally or on an untimed basis. The language therapists are encouraged to suggest any classroom modifications that might prove helpful. Other than these accommodations to the needs of the dyslexics, there is nothing done to single these students out from the rest. All attend chapel six days a week, all boys and girls dress according to a formal dress code, all regularly take part in squad work in which the student body handles school maintenance and housekeeping responsibilities. All take part in a wide range of interscholastic and recreational sports. Incidentally, the LD students have proved to be exceptionally good athletes. A recently hired art teacher has managed to engage the majority of the student body in creative aesthetic pursuits. Through choice, most students spend time in the sumptuously appointed library with its 8,000 volumes. Many also will go off camping by themselves in the mountains when the weekend weather is favorable.

Even though a crackdown on violations of the school rules in 1982 resulted in expulsions, a lot of trust and leeway is built into the Patterson program. Dorm rooms may look like disaster areas, notwithstanding periodic checks. Attire and behavior are outwardly that of ladies and gentlemen, but there is a casual familiarity that reflects a "down home" Southern upbringing, even though a fair proportion of the boarding students come from non-Southern states. There is also a jaunty insouciance about the student body which reflects its upper middle class origins.

Patterson School has had its money worries over the years, but it has fortunately weathered its various crises with fortitude and grace. An LD student who is potentially college material would find that his/her parents got their money's worth by enrolling him or her in this Carolina mountain sanctuary of academia.

THE SCHENCK SCHOOL
282 Mt. Paran Rd.
Atlanta, GA 30327

Private/Coed
Day
Enrollment 83
Ages 6-14

David Schenck struggled with dyslexia during his schooling years. In 1959, he founded his own school so that students with specific language disabilities could acquire the skills they needed to function successfully in a regular classroom. For the last 12 years, the school has been in a comfortable, rambling home in a woodsy, residential area of northwest Atlanta, Georgia.

Tuition for the 83 day students, aged 6 to 14, is $4,250 at the junior high level, $3,750 at the elementary level. Three or four scholarships are available. Prior to admission, a student must have been given psycho-educational diagnostic testing. The director and his assistant further screen each applicant by asking for written and oral work samples. If the child has a specific disability, would profit from a written language approach, has average or above intelligence and has no overriding emotional problems, he/she may be granted admission.

Once admitted, children are placed in groups according to age, social maturity and teacher testing results. No more than six are assigned to a room. The 19 full- and part-time teachers have, on the average, five years of classroom experience. The children mostly stay put in their small assigned classroom throughout the day because of the shortage of space. Interaction between students and their teachers is warm, casual and on a first-name basis. Few discipline problems are encountered. The classroom rules are made by the students at the beginning of each year. These primarily consist of restrictions against interfering with another student's work. A private conversation with the teacher usually solves any behavior problems, but some awareness activities or behavior modification techniques may be used.

Schenck uses an intense, modified Orton-Gillingham and Fernald multisensory approach to reading and writing. Each student also receives at least half an hour of one-to-one teaching daily. Reading mastery is achieved through writing stories. For developmental reading, and mathematics, each student has an individualized skill-building program. Work is checked constantly so that the child understands and corrects errors immediately; successes bring equally rapid praise and rewards.

Organization skills are emphasized at Schenck. Student-designed homework charts are filled in daily to ensure that the assignment is understood and done. Grammar rules, once explained, are organized in a notebook, and students create their own ways for remembering the exceptions. All new concepts are broken down into their component parts. In mathematics, for example, tables and problems are illustrated with concrete figures and steps. There are weekly tests in each subject, and every Friday folders go home to show how students have progressed. Parental feedback is encouraged. First graders may have up to 30 minutes of nightly homework; the older students may be expected to spend two hours unassisted at their desks.

Schenck has no gym; the students use a playground for physical fitness, soccer, basketball and volleyball. In bad weather, the lunchroom is cleared for the younger children. Older classes use a nearby gym twice weekly, but some days physical education time is spent playing board games. Art and music are taught weekly to first through fifth graders by classroom teachers. There is no science lab, although some scientific equipment is available. Because of space limitations plays are performed in the classroom.

Despite the lack of extras, Schenck students feel positively about their school experiences. The average stay is two years, after which students return to a regular program. Parents and pupils, however, feel free and like to come back to visit, borrow materials and seek help. Scores on the Stanford Achievement Test and the Iowa Test of Basic Skills, which are given each January and May, tell the major success story that Schenck has to share, namely that its approach works to remediate the academic deficiencies of the students who attend.

VANGUARD SCHOOL
2249 Highway 27 N.
Lake Wales, FL 33853

Private/Coed
Residential
Enrollment 140
Ages 6-19

Vanguard of Lake Wales, Florida, looks like a neat place. It is. Weeds and litter seem not to exist. The 140 boys and girls who call this 75-acre campus home for 180 school days (not including weekends) act calm, cool and collected, even when temperatures soar. Passersby along central Florida's State Highway 27 see an attractive cluster of 15 contemporary buildings, the groomed, grassy grounds and young people enjoying the outdoors.

This Vanguard is the outgrowth of a daytime educational program that began in 1959 in Paoli, Pennsylvania. Its intent has been to serve the needs of the "interjacent" child, the child with learning and coping-related disorders who was failing in school but who was ineligible or ill-suited for special education services available in his/her community. Mr. Harry Nelson, a faculty member and administrator at Paoli, was urged to start a residential satellite. After being assured of significant support in the central Florida area for such a venture, he undertook in 1965 the building of the second Vanguard program. He and this school have since become known for the successful way the salient social, emotional and instructional needs of Vanguard's youthful populace are met. Recommendations from satisfied parents and professional sources have meant a continuing increase in the number of applicants and referrals.

In 1983, Vanguard of Lake Wales became a separately incorporated, private institution. Its policies will evolve autonomously from those of its former affiliates. For instance, there will ultimately be no state-funded students enrolled, since Mr. Nelson prefers to design his own formulas for meeting the complex needs of each student rather than to adhere to governmental mandate.

Before being granted admission, students must have an on-campus interview and diagnostic testing. Approximately two thirds of those who submit admission requests and data are turned down or referred elsewhere. In selecting those students who attend, the critical determinant is the staff judgment that Vanguard is right for a particular child. The current student body ranges in age from 6 to 19 and is drawn from 19 states and 11 foreign countries. The cost of room and board is $11,800; there is only minimal scholarship assistance. A majority of the students come by plane, and those who arrive or depart on scheduled days are assisted by staff at either the Orlando or Tampa airports. Visits by family members during the school year are carefully regulated so as not to interfere with the ongoing program.

Vanguard is not a psychiatric treatment center, and yet its program is designed to address the underlying psychosocial barriers inhibiting the realization of a child's full potential. Little credence is accorded statistical measurements of intelligence, since, in the Vanguard view, scores are invalidated by emotional or behavioral factors. The 51-member staff works as a coordinated team to find the key to unlock each student's innate ability. After prioritizing a child's needs, collective decisions are made regarding the best mode and timetable for meeting these needs. The main difference between this approach and the usual IEP procedure is that emotional problems often receive first consideration. Reinteresting a child in learning and eliminating his/her passivity may be the first goal, or reducing a child's anxiety level so that he can function socially may be foremost. Once a student's attitude begins to change, he is ready to be challenged in the classroom.

An average of eight students is in each classroom. Everyone has for each basic subject a series of structured, sequential learning materals. Goals are reviewed and revised at midyear, but intermittently specialists will look over a child's folder and visit his/her classroom. If, in their opinion, the child needs special therapies outside of class, these will be arranged. Criterion-referenced testing and materials are such that child and teacher are constantly abreast of progress. The administration of standardized tests and four informal reading inventories during each school year further documents progress.

Mr. Nelson has assembled an amalgam of superior support staff; besides teachers of math, reading, language arts, social studies and science at the lower and middle levels, there are two reading specialists, two speech and language clinicians, two psychologists, a perceptual-motor specialist, two part-time librarians, two nurses, residential supervisors, a home and recreation coordinator and a principal. Additional support and supervisory staff serve the upper level where classes are departmentalized and a diverse complement of electives is offered. Ten of the 33 teachers are fully certified in LD, but all adapt their teaching techniques well to varied learning styles. Vanguard is currently revamping its career and vocational programs, and these promise to be an important program adjunct.

At Vanguard students receive a daily grade for citizenship, the cleanliness of their rooms and the quality of their academic work. These grades are averaged weekly, and the students with the highest averages on Friday get first choice of a variety of tempting, upcoming recreational outings and activities. The honor roll, which is posted weekly, is a powerful incentive also, since special privileges, including residence in the newly built honors dorm, are granted top academic performers. In all four dorms, a $50 vandalism fund is tapped each month to cover any damage that is unattributable to an individual. If no such damage occurs, the entire amount can be used by the dorm to plan something fun. Perhaps because of this ploy, graffiti and inoperative equipment were unseen. Also, the twin dormitory rooms were among the largest and most neatly kept of any schools visited.

At Vanguard, even the cooks and custodial help are involved in eliciting and rewarding positive accomplishments. The net effect is one of being part of a popular community project. There's no feeling of robot-like mechanization in the attitudes and behavior of Vanguard residents. It's a full and satisfying life, and many of the students who enter at ages older than 10 stay on until graduation. Depending on the student, a job or further studies may follow the award of a diploma. Annual follow-up studies of Vanguard graduates (more than 100 have graduated thus far) authenticate a successful adaptation to the "outside world."

WHITE OAK SCHOOL
8401 Leefield Rd.
Baltimore, MD 21234

Public/Coed
Day
Enrollment 344
Ages 2-13

Severely learning disabled youngsters in Baltimore County, Maryland, are luckier than many SLD students elsewhere, for in this sprawling county area outside of Baltimore City there are two public schools (level V) that meet their needs. The Chatsworth School in the northwest serves half of the county; White Oak, located east of the Beltway in a pleasant residential section near a county recreational area, serves the other half. These sister schools were purposely designed and built to accommodate children from infancy to age 13 who had speech and language problems and often emotional and/or behavioral difficulties. White Oak serves 344 boys and girls, a small portion of whom are hearing-impaired. They are transported from their homes, sometimes two and a half hour distances away, by 18 county buses. The typical enrollee is one of "average intelligence." He or she also responds typically with enthusiasm to this specialized school environment.

White Oak's two-story building is beautifully equipped and arranged. The PTA responds quickly to staff-expressed needs not met by the county. An invitingly open library/media center is the ground level hub. Around this core are classrooms, a diagnostic center, offices, a gym and a cafeteria. Downstairs are two "homey" apartments and observation rooms for the parent/infant classrooms. Throughout the school are prominent and beautiful displays of the children's work. The library and the music and art rooms are especially exciting activity centers.

127

Although built in 1977, three years after Chatsworth, White Oak is actually an extension of an earlier experiment at the six-room Woodvale School. The county had recognized, before the passage of P.L. 94-142, that many students in the district had what were called "behavioral learning problems" and needed special attention. The present White Oak principal and many of her staff taught at Woodvale; they helped draw up the plans for the handsome, large facility they now occupy.

When a visitor admires the White Oak physical plant, the principal agrees but adds, "It is finally only a building. Our best resource is our wonderful staff." The teachers are a diversified group, as is the student body. The staff may be novices or old-timers. Most are women; all have Special Education certification with training in either reading or LD. Many have obtained or are working on advanced degrees. The staff "love it here." Salaries are based on county schedules, turnover is low, and there is a strong in-service component. Other staff include a crisis resource team, a librarian, teachers for art, music and physical education and two guidance counselors. Volunteers and career opportunities students do some tutoring. The county provides an ancillary support staff of three child psychologists, a psychiatric social worker, an ophthalmologist, an audiologist, a speech/language pathologist and a pediatric consultant.

The county also maintains a unique diagnostic/prescriptive center here. Anyone from birth to age 21 may be served. Schools refer "enigmas" for an eight-week period of observation and clinical teaching within a class of six taught by two teachers and one aide. This spacious clinic includes two audiology suites. After the student's specific learning style or problem has been ascertained, the child returns whence he came with the clinic's recommendations for classroom follow-up and perhaps for a different placement within the local school.

The size of White Oak's student body has continually grown, and the average age of referred students has kept getting younger. The county believes in early diagnosis and remediation. For instance, parents in the county whose babies evince significant developmental problems may sign up for regular sessions in one of the simulated, three-roomed apartments where they are shown practical ways to augment their child's language development in the home. White Oak has a preschool for 3-to-5-year-olds. Playground equipment is geared increasingly to younger ages.

White Oak's curriculum is academically challenging; it matches that of the "feeder schools," since the school's purpose is to continue the thrust of the regular schools, get its students up to grade level and return them as expeditiously as possible to their local elementary or junior high school. The difference here is that the staff know how to adapt the regular classroom materials to LD needs and how to organize small group instruction. Approach is the key.

The typical student's learning disability is "involved," complex and/

or severe. A multisensory, individualized approach is used. Ability-grouped students may be placed in back-to-back classrooms totaling 16 or more; these are "team-organized" by two teachers and an itinerant aide. Positive rewards and individual organizational "helps," such as checklists, charts and green lights, are provided students so that they may stay "on task."

Classes that do well collectively throughout the week are announced over the intercom, and special treats, such as being allowed to watch a Friday afternoon movie, are given as rewards. Classroom frustrations are kept to a minimum. Children who temporarily lose control are referred to a crisis resource center, and during classtime there are group counseling sessions.

Besides the concentration on basic language and math skills and the attention paid to each student's modality strengths and weaknesses, there is an all-school focus on the arts. In the music classes, "Star Wars" has been adopted as a theme and carries over into all curricular areas. Within the library program, students are encouraged not only to read for pleasure, but also to make videotapes and filmstrips. The arts play a big part in White Oak's program.

Students are assigned homework in order to reinforce classroom work, but parents are not expected to help. Teachers send home weekly Friday folders, there are report cards four times a year, and an annual review plus other informal communications keeps parents cognizant of their child's progress.

White Oak is not complacent; the principal and staff are engaged in extensive research and development of their reading program. Last year a woodworking shop was equipped with help from local organizations and run part-time by a teaching aide; the principal is determined to find a replacement for this aide. A reading resources teacher is being sought, as well as personnel for directing the use of computers it is hoped will soon be installed.

The county's commitment to SLD students within its boundaries extends beyond the elementary age. A task force has studied the advisability of an upper *Level V* school. Presently, a transition school concept is being tried and watched closely at the home school. Those students who still need a protected school environment after age 13 are placed by the county in private schools through a cost-excess program. Most White Oak students, however, return to *Levels IV* and *III* with success; the minimum stay at White Oak is two years. The principal sees happy graduates and class valedictorians every Christmas and is already hearing from some Woodvale students now in college.

SCHOOLS OF THE MIDWEST

BREHM PREPARATORY SCHOOL
1245 E. Grand Ave.
Carbondale, IL 62901

Private/Coed
Day
Enrollment 45
Ages 12-21

The Brehm phenomenon heralds good tidings for the learning disabled. A former teacher whose son was dyslexic recognized the Midwest lacked a good residential school for LD adolescents. Mrs. Carol Brehm gathered together some of the top talent in the field of learning disabilities and then translated their concepts into a multimillion dollar private school on the outskirts of Carbondale, Illinois. In August of 1982, six modern buildings stood on what were once eight acres of cornfields, and 27 students and 21 full-time staff inaugurated the maiden school year of the Brehm Preparatory School. So well planned and constructed was this academic venture that an air of stability and success soon surrounded the place. The dorms have nearly reached a capacity of 48, staff has been increased, and additional campus buildings are planned.

Brehm School offers all the major content area courses required for an Illinois high school diploma, plus electives in typing, microcomputer programming, photography, woodworking, drafting and ceramics. Individual LD remedial support in the areas of reading, mathematics and language is provided daily. Four evenings a week there is a structured, two-hour, one-to-one tutorial program guided by specially hired persons from nearby Southern Illinois University (SIU). Beyond that, all residential, tutorial and instructional staff work as a team to ensure carryover of classroom learnings to the students' nonclasstime and living quarters.

Up to a dozen students live in each of the four residences. Within each is an apartment for the married couple whose responsibility it is to provide a homelike environment for the other occupants. Students prepare their own breakfasts, are served lunch and collaborate on planning and preparing the evening meal. House rules are the joint creation of the houseparents and students; curfews are "fair" and sleeping quarters are typically messy. The give-and-take between and among peers and adults is characterized by open doors, open smiles and considerate helpfulness. The past, woeful school histories of many of the young people currently enrolled contrast dramatically with their experience in this setting. In general, the aim of the school is to supply its students with the quality personnel, training, guidance and life experiences needed for liberation from past negative conditioning.

The overall effect of the Brehm environment is that of being in a grown-up community. Students have considerable freedom to do and be as they choose. Almost everyone is on a first-name basis. Access to the many cultural and recreational attractions of nearby SIU is a popular feature of the Brehm program. Few students risk losing off-campus privileges; withdrawing these for a designated time is the main means of control.

Throughout a typical school day, Brehm's outstandingly equipped computer room is usually jammed with students working on one of the nine machines. One dyslexic student who had not been "turned on" at two other highly touted schools for the learning disabled was so into computer programming that he had mastered the sophisticated contents of several trade journals. Other students, with the help of their English teacher, had compiled on the word processor a 20-page booklet of student-authored essays and comments. Others were playing games, graphing designs, completing study assignments or creating their own programs.

During regular classroom sessions between 8:30 AM and 3:30 PM, students discuss knowledgeably all manner of topics. In LD support classes, one-on-one instructional help is given in specific deficit areas. Students regularly drop in on the staff psychologist or school secretary for advice on personal problems or interests. Despite the easygoing orientation of the staff, an underlying discipline and structure govern all academic activities.

The student body is drawn from throughout the country. In 1982-1983, two students were funded. Nearly half are of post-secondary age, and of these a fair proportion are working on honing their skills for college entrance. Some are enrolled in courses part-time at SIU. Others are readying themselves for careers. The initial success of Brehm students in the competitive job market and the university milieu is promising. So appealing is this program to certain learning disabled individuals and their families that one 17-year-old dysgraphic school dropout, upon hearing from his parents of Brehm, drove nonstop from Colorado in a car he'd built himself in hopes he would meet the admissions criteria and be permitted to enroll.

The determination of eligibility for the program is made during a two-day psychological evaluation at Brehm for a fee of $525. The primary handicap must be a learning disability; secondarily there may be mild personal-social adjustment problems, neurological or perceptual-motor impairment and/or faulty earlier instruction. In order to accommodate the secondary problems, staff members provide individualized help in sensory integration and motor training (the facilities of SIU sports center and a nearby private recreation club are extraordinary facilities) and plenty of one-on-one counseling. The clinical resources of the university are easily accessible for diagnostic or therapeutic assistance not already available on the Brehm campus. A stiff maximum fee of $16,500 for tuition and boarding underwrites the school program.

Mrs. Brehm wanted the school bearing her name to reflect the state of the art of LD educational services. There's no question that the Brehm program is on the "cutting edge"; it will take a few years before the track records are established. Those interested in safe speculations concur that the future will show this school to be a winner.

THE CHURCHILL SCHOOL
7501 Maryland Ave.
St. Louis, MO 63105

Private/Coed
Day
Enrollment 73
Ages 8-16

The 73 neatly dressed boys and girls who crowd the staircase on route to their first period homerooms at the Churchill School in Clayton, Missouri, carry heavy book packs. There's no footdragging, slouching, jostling or rudeness; all seem eager to reach their destination. These youngsters, between 8 and 16 years of age, come to this private, ungraded day school from all over the greater St. Louis area. All have in common average or above intelligence and a specific language disability. Tuition is $8,500; no students are reimbursed by their school districts, but 12 percent have scholarship assistance. One youngster, misplaced previously in a school for the mentally retarded, has his tuition covered by two church parishes.

A typical day at Churchill begins with a 25-minute homeroom. These nine age-grouped classes concentrate on social skills and short-term goal setting techniques. During this period, an elected homeroom representative may also discuss student council deliberations. Afterwards, students go to ability-grouped classes in language arts, math, auditory/visual, social studies and motor skills. All have an individual 50-minute tutorial scheduled during the seven-hour school day. The day includes a 30-minute mid-morning break in which students either work out in the gym, study or have free social time. Children eat lunches brought from home at 1 PM in a basement-level "cafeteria;" adjacent is a self-contained, team-taught transition classroom that serves up to ten junior high level students planning soon to return to a more traditional school and curriculum.

Churchill started in 1979 as a summer session for 21 LD students. Within three years, a dynamic group of trustees had raised $360,000 with which to initiate a full-year program in leased second-floor space at the Maryland School. A 1.5 million dollar capital fund drive is under way to acquire a permanent 35,000 square foot home at the former Price School. Churchill owes its success thus far to (1) two St. Louis residents who spearheaded the school's founding, (2) Dr. Charles Drake, Headmaster of Landmark Schools, whose recommendations have shaped the program and (3) an unusually talented and imaginative staff of more than 30 teacher/tutors and administrators.

The one-to-one tutorial, plus the extremely low overall teacher-student ratio, the core of Churchill's program, allows the staff to concentrate on building individual linguistic skills. The students' tutors, who may also teach two classes of six pupils each, are charged with tackling their tutees' specific disability and with keeping track of all classroom progress. A 35-page evaluation is submitted to parents at the end of the school year which includes IEPs for all instructional areas. Each Friday, tutors tally and post a homework honor's list that recognizes all who have completed their week's worth of non-parent–assisted nightwork. Tutors alert staff during a daily faculty meeting of tutorial progress needing classroom reinforcement. Few, if any, "cracks" exist at Churchill for students to fall through.

The school rejects the "pay-off" practice of token rewards for achievement. Only one youngster is on the "point system." During the admissions intake procedure, applicants must individually commit themselves to working with the school's upfront remedial objective of returning to traditional classrooms within two years.

Learning-avoidance habits do not last long because of an unusually effective motivational ploy used in the 47-minute motor skills class. Here, students must run vigorously every other day. If they don't run, they can't stay at Churchill. In developing healthy cardiovascular systems, they also win aerobic points, enjoy mileage club participation and become proud of themselves. On alternate days, emphasis is placed on seasonal sports, such as karate, baseball, soccer and basketball. A videotape machine helps students see which and how sports skills need developing. School teams periodically compete against other schools and the faculty. One 13-year-old master-avoider flew apart at the running requirement, but, after two weeks, his resistance broke down; his classroom negativism of earlier days vanished with acceptance of the motor skills regimen.

Public speaking breeds fear in many, but not at Churchill. The social studies and science curriculum forges a unique link between written and oral language; it stresses an organized, step-by-step approach to decoding, the use of maps and reference materials and the formal oral presentation of ideas. All Churchillians participate in a spring speech contest. Three represented the school in a metropolitan forensics event. In class, students sytematically and constructively evaluate each other on their speech content and presentation style.

Processing skills necessary for intelligent public speaking are covered in the auditory/visual class. The material may include sequencing, tracking, closure or memory training. Language classes stress grammar and composition. Math concentrates on basic concepts and skills and often requires daily drill. Reading comprehension is an across-the-board objective; the school's curricular materials and tutors' encouragement of independent reading yield significant progress as shown in standardized test results. In the transition class, students use standard texts, receive numerical grades and are expected to internalize scanning, questioning and reviewing techniques. Learning how to learn is the basic emphasis in this experimental program.

Churchill doesn't baby its students. Indeed, the staff-student interaction is remarkably fraternal. This relationship is fostered during an all-school three-day autumn camp-out during which rappelling, orienteering, breadmaking, macramé, initiative games, archery and tie-dying are taught and learned together.

The Churchill plan has evolved quickly, thanks to staff dynamics and a forward-looking board. According to the school director, school success may best be measured by the complaint-free response of its "graduates" and their parents. Of 30 former students, half received supportive, school-provided tutoring during their first mainstream semester, but only five were getting extra help after four months. Years may pass before the full value of a Churchill infusion is fully documented, but initial indicators are extraordinarily promising.

COLUMBUS HIGH SCHOOL
3231 W. 95th Street
Waterloo, IA 50701

Parochial/Coed
Day
Enrollment 812
Ages 14-18

The Columbus High School LD program is essentially "the resource room"— with a difference. It works the way educational planners dream it might. Even the students endorse it. No stigma is attached to participation. This program is available in a comprehensive, four-year Catholic high school, a well-maintained, attractive facility located in a desirable section of Waterloo, Iowa.

The school principal, the Rev. Mr. Walter Brunkan, is an affable, easy-going and extremely capable administrator who has been at Columbus since its beginnings in 1958. Father Brunkan is deservedly proud of the school's plant and program; the evident " feeling of family" is largely of his making.

Currently attending Columbus High are 812 boys and girls. Tuition is negotiable but averages about $700 per pupil; diocesan support helps cover more than half of the cost. In 1982-1983, 39 students were LD. They were eligible by virtue of meeting the Iowa criteria for receiving support in a multicategorical resource room. Frequent program evaluations have established that few, if any, of the 39 felt embarrassed by their placement in the program. One pass-fail graduation credit is earned for a full year assignment. The entire LD program, however, is an adjunct to the regular classroom program, inasmuch as all LD students are mainstreamed. The two LD teachers and an available reading specialist help with class assignments on an "individualized but not individual" basis during the resource room periods. They also serve as facilitators for teachers of the regular subject matter.

Early in September, the LD teachers send a confidential list to any regular faculty who will have LD students in their classes. Relevant, specialized information regarding such matters as the students' reading, writing and math abilities, their organizational and note-taking skills and their learning styles is also shared. Of prime importance to the success of this program is the high degree of ongoing cooperation between the special education and subject matter teachers. Both groups welcome opportunities to confer privately on ways each may help facilitate student learning. From time to time, the regular teachers are asked to write brief special reports about an LD student's progress, test scores, homework and behavior.

Another form utilized is the "IEP — Modification of Class Assignments," which specifies just how the subject matter teacher assists the LD student. Examples are reading text chapters aloud, providing study guides or end-of-chapter questions in reading, having extra time for written assignments, borrowing class notes from another student and copying them, writing assignments without grade reduction for bad spelling or handwriting, monitoring student progress by using a contract grading or a checklist reporting system or by holding regularly scheduled student-teacher conferences, shortening a project or research paper, modifying testing procedures or utilizing alternate materials at lower reading levels.

Two other forms are used to help assess student progress and to effect improvement. One is the student status report that parents of all Columbus students receive. The second is an evaluation form that the LD students are periodically asked to complete; the eight questions and multiple-choice answers encourage a good critique of the resource program.

The director of the program is enthusiastic, experienced and LD certified. Her full-time assistant lacks this certification. Additional specialized staff serve the Columbus program through the auspices of an Iowa state agency called Area VII. They administer the test battery required for admission into the program. The staff at Columbus subsequently administers the Shaw/Hiele Individual Computational Skills Program and the Woodcock Reading Mastery Test, the results of which are used in developing IEP objectives. The Area VII staff includes a psychologist and social worker who come once a week, a speech clinician who comes 2½ days each, and an occupational therapist and audiologist who come upon request. Red Cross volunteers and students from the University of Northern Iowa assist the LD teachers, the latter for field experience. There is also a peer/tutoring program that matches LD and non-LD students as study partners.

Parents, staff, administration and the students themselves commend the Columbus High School LD program. The LD students are the chief beneficiaries, but the academic faculty act truly appreciative of the sharing of expertise: they realize the resulting modification of teaching strategies in the classrooms have effectively minimized the academic frustrations of all students. Other small schools would do well to emulate this simple, uncomplicated and low-cost program model.

COVE SCHOOL
1100 Forest Ave
Evanston, IL 60602

Private/Coed
Day
Enrollment 84
Ages 6-20

Cofounded in 1947 by Drs. Alfred A. Strauss and Laura Lehtinen Rogan, Cove School still enjoys a preeminent place among schools for the learning disabled. Not only was Cove the first such school to exist, but also it has never lost that pioneering spirit which brought it into being, although for the past few years difficult accommodations to such practical realities as income and expenditures have had to be made. Dr. Rogan still functions as clinical director and primary consultant, but much of her time is now devoted to completion of the Cove School Reading Program publications. Her guidance and inspiration quietly animate all that happens at Cove. Day-to-day exigencies are the responsibility of Dr. Lannie LeGear, associate director, and Dr. Theodore Kolesnik, principal. The staff of 22 full- and part-time teachers share an esprit comparable to that of the adults in a loving, hard-working family. It is this cohesiveness which is the main attribute of the Cove program.

Now located less than a mile south of downtown Evanston, Illinois, in a converted "landmark" mansion, Cove serves from September until June as a day school for 84 boys and girls, aged 6 to 20, who come from posh distant suburbs as well as the Chicago inner city. About half are tuition-reimbursed by local districts. The ethnic and socioeconomic diversity of the student body makes for a sprightly spontaneity. It gets boisterous at times, especially during passing periods and on field trips, but the youngsters recognize this behavior as "letting off steam." Most children show genuine respect and caring for one another; destructive peer pressure is minimal. Most Cove students have never felt good about themselves or others before, and they feel strangely lucky to be out of "the maelstrom of the mainstream" and into the temporary therapeutic haven which is Cove. Cove is indeed a haven of last resort for the high schoolers. For the others, a return within an average of 2½ years to their regular school district is the pattern.

Any student of average or above intelligence who has been identified by an outside agency as LD and whose acting out is deemed manageable is eligible for admission at any time of the school year. Upon submission of the requisite reports and histories, prospective students are screened at Cove for a $100 fee. Acceptance is dependent upon the staff's determination that the child can be significantly helped and that there is currently a group into which the child will fit, based on his/her age, size, personality, social maturity and achievement level. This very individual-ized evaluation illustrates the child-centeredness as well as the practicality of Cove's orientation. A bright nonreader, for instance, who was nearly seven feet tall and 17 years old was enrolled at the same time a girl of 13 with marginal LD problems was denied admission.

At $4,700, Cove's tuition costs are quite reasonable. The well-maintained, handsome building is filled to capacity. Small group tutoring takes place in the equivalent of closets. The school's second and third floor classrooms of small to adequate size each contain a maximum of eight students. Budget deficits, however, have been curtailing expendi-tures for equipment, materials, program and salaries. The set of worn-out weights in the multipurpose gym is in nearly constant use. The books in the library attest to heavy usage, and many of them are on loan from the public library. The librarian directs a commendable program fostering the reading of good literature and the development of research skills. Students are not constantly supervised because teachers believe in gradually giving them more and more opportunities to exercise responsible judgment. Teachers use any free time to plan lessons, brainstorm dilemmas, evaluate student work and supply instant feedback to those who have made progress or need redirection. A social worker, an art therapist, a visual motor specialist and a speech/language therapist come on a part-time basis. Fourteen of the 22 staff are LD certified. The staff discussions at lunchtime and at coffee breaks are excitingly intense,

137

as all present seem only to talk about the latest instructional breakthrough or the need to adjust the program of someone who is still blocked. Teachers are drained at the end of the day, for not only are all involved with all students, but also teachers must discuss and work through the issues associated with any child's misconduct that requires that he/she be sent out of class. Children think they are quite on their own at Cove, but actually they are in a structured, supervised environment at all times.

Many, but not all, Cove students go on to college. For students at Cove, the counseling is extensive and realistic, and all are made cognizant of their strengths and weaknesses. Parents are an integral part of this sharing. In some cases, especially during those "crisis" times when a child is about to make a cognitive leap, school-to-home communication is daily. Homework does not involve the parents, but it, like all the other instructional practices, is designed to enable the student to integrate and internalize the skills and attitudes necessary to meet the demands of future situations. During the first two thirds of one's enrollment at Cove, primary emphasis is placed on basic skill acquisition and self-esteem enhancement. The latter third is usually spent on catching up in the student's various academic subject matter areas so that he/she may function effectively at grade level in his/her former school district. That might or might not be in the college-bound track. Cove staff members act as advocates and counselors to students, their new teachers and their families during the transition back into the mainstream.

In 1947, Dr. Rogan wrote in one of the earliest books on learning disabled students: "Teaching is in part concerned with making available in suitable form and at the appropriate developmental level those areas of human knowledge which experience or tradition have judged essential. With guidance and positive motivation, learning progresses as naturally as physical growth." Fortunately Dr. Rogan never gave up attempting to prove the validity of that statement. She is still writing the books on and for the learning disabled, and Cove is a national resource center with landmark status comparable to that of the mansion housing the school. At some point, perhaps the dedicated staff can point to more than job satisfaction as their primary remuneration, and Cove can become less dependent on the vagaries of state funding.

MINER SCHOOL
1101 E. Miner
Arlington Heights, IL 60004

Public/Coed
Day
Enrollment 300
Ages 5-21

Miner School is unique among the schools described in this book in that it is fairly large, it exclusively serves LD students from kindergarten through high school, and it is public and therefore "free." An uninformed bystander might conclude from a quick glance at Miner that this was another typical, traditional school. But he might be puzzled by the large and irregular assortment of school buses that come constantly throughout the school day to drop off or pick up students. The children's disparate ages and sizes might be perplexing also; the students are between 5 and 21 years of age. But the natural camaraderie of the 300 students and 78 staff members; the studious concentration within all 21 classes; and the attractive, well-maintained building and grounds convey a feeling of thriving normalcy. Actually, despite the classification of the entire student body as severely disabled and the exorbitant expense of the bus shuttling, Miner is flourishing according to standard norms of success.

Students at Miner are transported to and from their schools and homes within ten separate districts under the aegis of the Northwest Suburban Special Education Organization (NSSEO), the regional special education cooperative which serves the northwestern Chicago suburbs from Schaumburg to Buffalo Grove, a geographic area of 142 square miles. Some students may attend Miner from 8:15 AM to 3 PM, but most attend their home school for a mainstreamed portion of each day. Not only is it the philosophical purpose of Miner to provide sufficient academic remediation for its students to enable them to succeed where once they failed in their regular school, but the means of ensuring that such progess occurs is a gradual and carefully articulated one with the feeder school. Once a student can manage successfully in 50 percent of his regular classes, he returns full-time, but he may return after school to Miner for extra help.

Established in 1979 and housed since 1980 in a former junior high in Arlington Heights, Illinois, the Miner LD Center originated in response to a needs assessment survey conducted by district staff. Results indicated that despite a continuum of LD services in each member school district there were still many children whose learning handicaps and attitudes prevented them from "keeping up." In essence, this condition is the basic criterion for acceptance at Miner. Besides poor adaptive behavior and low average functioning, motor impairment or multiple handicaps often exist, but these latter difficulties are considered secondary. Recently, more specific eligibility requirements have been readied for board approval. Standardized and criterion-referenced academic testing are used to measure progress and to determine when a

139

student's functioning approximates that of his peers in his home district so that reentry preparations may begin.

At Miner, the principal has personal charge of all staff supervision, student records and building administration. Under her are a mainstream coordinator, a psychoeducational diagnostician, two psychologists (and one intern), one social worker, three language therapists, one part-time occupational therapist and a prevocational coordinator, as well as teachers, aides, student teachers, volunteers, secretaries and custodial staff.

This staff is organized into four teams, one for each level — primary, intermediate, junior high and high school. At the lower levels, the math and reading programs are carefully sequenced and individualized. These levels are in self-contained classrooms. The high schoolers have a semi-departmentalized curriculum, and the basics are taught through a variety of instructional materials emphasizing their practical application. A variety of electives is offered the older students, including driver education, shop, office skills, home economics and photography. An average class might contain 13 students, one teacher and an aide, but some instructional situations might have only one or two students. At least once a week, a language therapist and the psychologist and/or social worker separately visit each class; they work on receptive and expressive language or social adjustment and self-concept. Basic and adaptive physical education are offered twice weekly. The spacious library is primarily used as a resource area; the computer, reference books, board games, plus fiction and nonfiction from the days of Miner Junior High, are kept here. Teaching and teaming practices such as these reflect the school's intent to provide an innovative, cost-effective and managerially sound program of remediation and self-actualization for each student. Behavior modification programs, ranging from positive reinforcement to assertive discipline, are different for each group. The staff views homework as an important adjunct to academic work, both as a means of reinforcement and as a means of learning responsibility. Parents are not expected to help or get into a struggle with their children over assignments. In such areas, considerable resources are made available to students' families. Just as the teachers draw upon the expertise of educational authorities through regular in-service activities, so also do the parents avail themselves of the counseling and programs offered them. There is a minimum of five annual parental conferences, and weekly rap sessions are well attended in the evenings. This interaction accounts in part for the mutual receptivity to outside participation in the extensive extracurricular activities at Miner. Community volunteers are often present, and their projects are coordinated by a district staff person.

Many school-sponsored social and recreational groups exist at Miner; a Girl Scout troop is active; an Explorer unit goes camping and even pilots airplanes. There are school dances, student council activities, a uniformed cheerleader squad, a chess and checker tournament, fine arts assemblies, student-faculty sports contests and intramural and inter-mural competitions. Older students take part in a wide variety of prevocational and vocational activities, such as helping with building construction off-campus and managing a cafeteria food service program. There is a Miner graduation ceremony, even though diplomas are awarded by the home school. At this occasion, students spontaneously avow how Miner has helped them; hugs, tears and promises to return abound. As one new freshman stated, even though she'd experienced considerable teasing about being bused to this different school, "Miner's all right!"

Miner keeps growing. It has the space to expand, the regional population growth to ensure a source of enrollees, a board that is convinced of the merits of the Miner concept, and an able administrative staff. Already Miner has achieved recognition from the Council of Exceptional Children for its innovative program. Although this is possibly the affordable answer for some whose public school program is not beneficial, potential move-ins are advised that referral to and acceptance at Miner are decisions made within each feeder district, not at Miner. Even so, the systematic and thorough processing of data on all students potentially, currently or formerly enrolled at Miner is especially commendable and reflects well on the intent of the Miner staff to go beyond the minimal intent of the law as found in PL 94-142. There seems to be the feeling that all students who need the special environment and help that Miner provides can and will be welcome.

THE SPRINGER EDUCATIONAL FOUNDATION *Private/Coed*
2121 Madison Rd. *Day*
Cincinnati, OH 45208 *Enrollment 178*
Ages 6-14

Everything is under control at the Springer School of Cincinnati, Ohio. Budgetary matters seem to elicit nary a fret. Corridors and classrooms are quiet and orderly, and the students seem particularly engrossed in their various learning pursuits. There is even an imperturable quality to outdoor recess. Such calm usually does not hold sway in a 2½ story school building for one hundred learning disabled children between 6 and 14. A century's worth of long range planning may account for the lack of frenzy; it also serves to explain the program's distinctiveness.

The Springer Educational Foundation grew out of a sizable bequest in 1884 for the creation of a parish school in conjunction with the city's

141

downtown cathedral. Sixty years later, Springer became the archdiocesan special education school and was run by the Sisters of Charity. Then in 1969, the school opted to limit its enrollment to learning disabled children and in 1979 to become "affiliated" with the County Board of Education as it had earlier done with the University of Cincinnati. In 1971, the school was incorporated as a public, non-sectarian foundation for the benefit of children with special learning difficulties. This quasi-public relationship over the years enabled Springer to take advantage of some of the "free" services of the State of Ohio while still retaining its status as a private school. Currently 23 percent of the school's income is derived from an annual fund drive and endowment income; nearly $40,000 of this amount goes toward scholarship assistance for tuition which is otherwise $4,288 per year.

The diagnostic clinic is just one of three especially noteworthy attributes of the Springer Foundation. Referrals come from all manner of professional sources throughout the Greater Cincinnati area, as well as parents. The purpose of the clinic is to analyze the specific problems of children suspected of being "learning disabled" and to prescribe adjustments based on these findings. These recommendations might or might not be that the child attend Springer. If the child is to be considered for admission at Springer or wishes to receive a full evaluation, the cost is $595. He or she is scheduled for ten consecutive mornings in a separate diagnostic classroom setting during which time the clinician will continue with the work and materials of the child's regular classroom. Afterwards, there are visitations to and staffing conferences with the child's regular school and his teachers. School placement decisions are made after conferences with the child's parents, and follow-up arrangements are made.

Besides undergoing this extensive evaluation, the child must have an IQ of at least 90 to be admitted. Each will have an individually designed educational program and be placed in a classroom which may contain up to 12 children. The number of ancillary support staff in addition to the 23 regular staff, of whom 15 are fully certified in LD, is such that the actual teacher-pupil ratio is close to one to four. Interns and more than 40 trained volunteers assist in the classroom, clinic and sports programs. Art, music, physical education, the library, speech therapy, visual integration, sensory integration and psychological counseling are available at all three instructional levels. The school is beautifully equipped with an auditorium-gymnasium, lockers, showers, a science lab, music and art rooms and all the perquisites of a modern comprehensive high school. Students have been heard often saying, "Gee, it's just like a real school." The boys' basketball teams, the reserve and varsity cheerleaders, the wrestling tournaments, the volleyball, soccer and track competitions, plus the annual athletic banquet at which all participants receive letters, help strengthen this impression.

Reeducation is the second noteworthy facet and strong point at Springer. An eclectic approach is used at all levels; but nothing is hodgepodge about the way materials, objectives and strategies are selected. There are, for example, 50 different texts in the basic reading program. Each child has an individual assignment for each subject each day. Within the various classrooms study carrels may be facing the wall, but children work on improving concentration so that they may earn the right to move into the center of the room. Disciplinary actions are the responsibility of the individual teacher, but misbehavior seems rarely a problem. Inasmuch as the goal of the school is to enable the student to return to a conventional classroom, the science, arts, social studies and physical education classes are taught in a traditional group way. To whatever extent possible, all classrooms are homogeneous. Because each student's level of achievement is different, however, even group activities allow for different modes of participation. Once a child is deemed ready in January to return the following September to a regular school, the child is placed in a higher output situation, often requiring up to 2½ hours of nightly homework. Also at this point, the liaison work begins with the school or schools to which the student might return. This reentry feature marks the third facet of the Springer program which sets it apart from other learning disability institutions.

Few other schools work so arduously to help parents find the appropriate school to which a child should go *after* Springer. Often five alternatives will be explored before a decision is made. Thereafter, the liaison coordinator continues as the child's advocate in his subsequent school setting. It is said that "Once a Springer student, always one!"

Another reason for the tenacity of the Springer bond, besides the continuous follow-up done on those who leave, is the remarkable spirit and personality of Sister Marianne Van Vurst, the school's administrator and prime mover since the days of the 60s. She had the foresight to know when and why change was necessary and to make adequate provisions beforehand so that there were no unnecessary disruptions in the educational programs of the school. She negotiated with the Archdiocese to buy the Marian High School and the three-acre Hyde Park property on which the present school is situated; she obtained city-wide support for a private learning disabilities school, and she will establish one day satellite schools serving older age children. She sets the tone which ensures that at Springer everything is under control.

SUMMIT SCHOOL
611 E. Main Street
Dundee, IL 60118

Private/Coed
Day
Enrollment 144
Ages 6-19

At a recent gala homecoming given by the staff and board of Summit School in Dundee, Illinois, the 150 attending alums shared aloud personal accounts of their academic and vocational success since Summit days. Ruth Tofanelli, the school's executive director, was "tingly" with sentiment and pride. She recalled the severely learning disabled twin girls whose father had asked her in 1967 to give his daughters schooling; they had been ousted from a public school first grade. She had agreed to try. Mrs. Tofanelli, the twins and six other students met in rented church space on a half-day basis throughout the ensuing year. Little did this teacher expect that this trial program would evolve into an avant-garde day school, a diagnostic clinic and summer residential camps. Nor was it anticipated that this same school would house a privately funded gifted program, an after-school tutorial service, EEG equipment, teacher training workshops and a remarkable preschool. Perhaps the father who first broached the idea of starting a class had such notions in mind. As President Emeritus of the Summit Board, he has spearheaded all of these developments. Direct credit for all the homecoming success stories belongs, however, to Mrs. Tofanelli. She accepted "misfits" others turned away. One "grad" whom referring psychologists said had an IQ no higher than 55 was functioning very intelligently in a student nursing program. Another "retarded" Summit departee was finishing with his class at Annapolis.

Summit School is housed in a modified and enlarged former professional office building, notable for its starkly modern and functional appearance. Boys and girls from preschool through high school age come mostly by bus from nearly all of the outlying Chicago suburbs; and every afternoon between 12:30 and 1 they leave to return to their regular school, home or job. This five-hour "day" and the afternoon mainstreaming have been the subject of two court battles, each of which has been settled in Summit's favor. State-funding pays for 110 of the 126 learning disabled students; this mandates a tuition rate of $6,445.40. Summit's intensive remediation allows most students to return full-time to their regular school within two years. A four-year long research project at the school led to the controversial conclusion that fully 90 percent of LD students could be helped by appropriate pharmacalogical intervention.

A new experimental preschool (modeled on the theories and practices of Suzuki) in 1983 served 16 students for $5.00 daily; the children were fluent in French and Japanese, were knowledgeable regarding the arts and were reading at the fifth grade level. Conceivably, Mrs. Tofanelli will revise her program emphases completely in light of

144

this preschool experiment. Up until now, the premise has always been the same – namely that Summit would daily look at what the child did, what he didn't do, why he didn't do it, how his problem could next be approached, and so on until the key could be found. Also, the prevailing ethos has been the spirit that is expressed in the phrase, "Let's do it!" Most of the youngsters get quickly coopted into this attitudinal community.

The full Summit staff includes 30 fully certified LD teachers, thus allowing a teacher-pupil ratio of less than one to five, mathematically speaking, although the average class size is eight or nine. The basics in reading, math and writing are emphasized, and all curricular materials and techniques are individualized according to the prescribed needs of each student.

One sample junior high classroom began at 8:30 AM with a pledge of allegiance, followed by housekeeping tasks and a current events discussion. Math work came next, and then the students concentrated on reading. Although the makeup of the class changed as some left or returned from separate specialized activities, the six to eight present stayed on task beautifully. A teacher-designed vocabulary recognition game engaged all as participants despite varying degrees of skills and abilities. The room was carpeted, windowless, soundproofed and uncluttered; the simple furniture was flexibly arranged to enhance concentration. The teacher kept close track of all independent work and provided instant correction and feedback. On the blackboard was described a five-step procedure whereby one check for misconduct required that the miscreant do 75 sit-ups or push-ups, three checks meant a half hour in a quiet room, and five meant a telephone call to the parents. Restlessness and disinterest vanished quickly as the teacher modified her instructional game plan at the first signs of frustration. A light-hearted approach, gentle humor and formidable energy were her allies as she led her students to accomplish the objectives she had in mind.

At the secondary level, which is semi-departmentalized, the dean functions as department chairman and disciplinarian, but his real role is to facilitate an attitudinal change on the part of his charges. Helpful to him, as well as the lower level supervisor and the staff, are the services of two psychologists, one social worker, two occupational therapists, three motor specialists, one psychoeducational diagnostician, four language and speech therapists, and the director of the medical clinic. The swimming pool, gymnasium and "weight room" at Summit are gorgeous, modern and ideally suited to the school's remedial and recreational physical education program. Teachers may participate in the incentive program which rewards monetarily those who plan and implement major curricular changes. Afternoons are usually free for planning, communication and interaction with parents and students' regular school teachers.

Meetings with parents are monthly and mandatory. Teachers take a very active role in supervising their students' reentry to the mainstream. Sometimes a child isn't really "let go" until he receives his high school diploma, although the high school may be fifty miles alway.

Mrs. Tofanelli likes being called a "revolutionary." She would like to see American education revamped so that all students receive early enough the individual attention and intellectual stimulation they need in order to realize their potential. Summit has been designated by the Federal government an observation site. Undoubtedly educators and the general public will hear more before long from this spokesperson for change.

SCHOOLS OF THE FAR WEST

ARENA SCHOOL
1223 Court St.
San Rafael, CA 94901

Private/Coed
Day
Enrollment 11
Ages 6-14

Arena addresses a critical need in the LD population with its comprehensive program for the severely learning handicapped child. Established in 1972, and originally overseen by John Arena, well-known educator and publisher (Academic Therapies), this school concentrates on developing coordination, perceptual skills and communicative ability while providing a sound academic program.

Arena once served 40 children. Because of California funding cutbacks, there are now only 11 students aged 6 to 14, all of whom have their $4,000 to $6,000 tuition district-reimbursed. These students occupy a rather forlorn and empty school building in noisy, downtown San Rafael, California. Two elementary classrooms, one for the lower and one for the upper level, and rooms for occupational therapy, motor skills development and visual training are more than adequate. Many rooms are not in use. On staff are two teachers who are fully credentialed in the learning handicap field and four skilled therapists with advanced training in their respective disciplines — occupational therapy, educational diagnostic therapy, vision therapy and motor skills development. No longer does Arena serve high school age students because the severity of the emotional problems of these students was too much for the staff to handle.

Required for admission are submission of prior academic and psychological testing results and a visit to Arena by the child and his parents. Each staff specialist later screens and evaluates accepted students for visual perception, sensory motor integration, academic functioning and gross motor skills. Standardized testing occurs four times a year, and parents attend at least three conferences yearly.

Arena believes that before a child can achieve basic academic mastery, his learning processes must be enhanced. The therapists work on a one-to-one basis with these processing modalities deficits. For instance, ten of the Arena pupils require visual therapy. Other children at Arena typically perform at the very bottom in performance testing for their age level. These are not Little League All-Stars; they need extensive help in motor skills development. The full-time specialist in this area uses the Feldenkris technique of movement patterning to improve motor functioning.

The reading, writing and arithmetic instruction is highly individualized. Several methodologies are employed for the widely disparate Arena student body ranging from non-readers to a computer whiz. Volunteers from Dominican College of Marin and San Francisco State provide valuable classroom assistance. Although Arena doesn't provide many academic options — no library, labs, fine arts, shop — the children take many trips into San Francisco for cultural and recreational enrichment. They play with a computer and are fortunate in having close to a one-to-one teacher-pupil ratio, a highly specialized support staff and an unusually strong skills development program.

THE CHARLES ARMSTRONG SCHOOL
360 LaCuesta Dr.
Menlo Park, CA 94025

Private/Coed
Day
Enrollment 212
Ages 4-18

"Slingerland" is not likely to be a part of an everyday vocabulary unless one decides to have a child attend the Armstrong School. Slingerland is a multisensory teaching strategy integrating the three

147

sensory modalities. No other teaching method is used at the school. Beth Slingerland, who worked with Anna Gillingham and Samuel Orton, adapted their system, designed for a one-to-one tutoring situation, for classroom use. It is quite a sight to watch 17-year-old high school students writing in the air as they spell out loud the word presented to them by their teacher.

The school, founded in 1968, serves children from kindergarten through high school at two sites in the San Francisco and East Bay areas. Unfortunately, Armstrong is a day program with no facilities for boarding. Many of its 212 boys and girls live too far away to commute and must find suitable housing in the area.Tuition is $5,000 to $6,300.

Admission is granted to children with a specific language disability (dyslexia) on the basis of a full-scale WISC-R and successful participation in the summer tutoring program. Students must be tested by their home school districts or an outside agency, exhibit no primary emotional problems, have normal intelligence and sit still for the rigorous one and a half to two hours of Slingerland language classes each day.

Because this is an intensive language therapy school, a good part of the day is alloted to reading and language classes. And because the staff feels there is not nearly enough time for the basics, there are few of the extras usually associated with good private schools. Armstrong places little emphasis on the creative; it has no enrichment courses, no inter-scholastic sports program, no marching band, no cheerleaders. Children are there to learn to read. The high school offers social studies, mathematics, science, computer training and typing, while the lower school follows a regular elementary program. Each child is placed in an ungraded classroom according to his ability and peer group. As all the teachers are Slingerland-trained, children are exposed to a consistent teaching approach believed to provide critical continuity. The 20 classrooms, originally designed for 30 students, are more than adequate for classes of 12. Plenty of extra space allows for separate reading, work and art areas. Many children's projects are on display in the rooms. The large library is well stocked with reading materials and seems to be a gathering place for high school students.

According to the Slingerland philosophy, the best remediation is early remediation. Therefore, Armstrong is very excited about a new program recently developed for preschoolers. Eight "little-ones," as they are affectionately called, attend the school's preventitive program. The staff feels that early diagnosis and remediation spare a child failure later in a regular classroom.

In addition to their training in the Slingerland method, all of the classroom teachers hold California handicapped credentials, and six of the 23 faculty have earned a Master's degree. The support staff is not extensive; included for both schools are speech and language specialists, a librarian, an art teacher and physical education teachers.

Slingerland summer schools and Slingerland teacher training

workshops are held at the school under the auspices of the nearby College of Notre Dame. It is Armstrong's goal to establish the Slingerland method in the public schools, and to this end the school acts as a summer teacher training institute.

One way of describing this school might be to say it's single-minded. And all minds are grounded in the Slingerland method! In answering the question of whether strict adherence to this one method works, Armstrong claims it has considerable success, probably due to the careful screening process which is more selective than in other California LD schools. The Armstrong and the Slingerland method work well for those the school chooses. A glowing tribute was given by a lovely high school girl who lives with a family in the area so that she can attend Armstrong: "...nobody knows what it is like not being able to read...you walk around afraid people will find out...the biggest thrill for me came when I was able to go into a grocery store and read the labels on the cans."

CENTER FOR EDUCATION
13321 Garden Grove Blvd.
Garden Grove, CA 92643

Private/Coed
Day & Tutoring
Enrollment 40
Ages 6-20

This unusual little school, another of the many new LD facilities in California, is administered by a high powered husband and wife team which combines expertise and enthusiasm to make the Center a diversified but high-quality operation. The Center has a dual program; one for the mildly to severely learning disabled student and a second for those who are achieving at grade level or above but whose parents are unwilling to put them back into a regular school situation. The parents and directors believe these children would not receive anything like this highly individualized approach "where students' strengths are explored and their weaknesses considered" in the larger classrooms of the public or private school where the curriculum is the same for everyone. The directors feel this mixture benefits both groups of children. In fact, they feel so strongly about this program that they have taken their own children out of a gifted class at a private school and enrolled them at the Center. The 13 non-LD high school and elementary level students act as role models for the 27 LD students; the latter are in three separate classes with one teacher and an aide. Tuition is between $500 and $800 a month, depending on the program.

Children with serious behavior problems are not accepted unless the directors are convinced that the behavior results from the frustration associated with inappropriate programming and that this behavior can be modified. This policy is clearly stated in the parent interview. Before admission is granted, the child must spend a day at the school so that he can be observed by the staff. As only six of the 27 students are funded by their school districts and since funded students are primarily ones with behavior problems, the Center appeals primarily to the private sector, a fact which contributes to enrollment selectivity.

The school is located in a business mall and is surrounded by a concrete parking lot. Classes are held in what were once office suites, and, while they are not spacious, there is adequate room for the eight to ten children in each class. Although there are no such amenities as science labs, computer terminals, a gymnasium and workshops, the school does have a small library/curriculum center which doubles as a lunchroom. Students use the local library, and physical education classes are held at a neighboring YMCA or nearby park.

The academic program follows the standard elementary and high school curriculum, with work in the content areas being treated primarily as an extended reading lesson. The units of study are designed to revolve around the standard public school curriculum using age-appropriate LD materials. The specific techniques and materials used for reading instruction are chosen according to each student's mode of learning. The Center is not wed to any one method, for it has found its eclectic approach to be an efficient and effective way to deal with its diverse population. For those children who have auditory based deficits and who have not learned to read by the standard phonetic approach, the Fernald whole word, multisensory approach is employed.

Instead of offering discrete courses designed to promote sensory integration or to resolve perceptual problems, the staff will incorporate into a student's curriculum appropriate remedial techniques. For example, a child may need help with the visual motor skills of writing, but his program will be designed so that his inability to write will not hinder his ability to achieve in other areas.

All teachers meet the same educational requirements as teachers in the public schools. The staff is experienced, and, according to the director, there has been very little turnover since 1978. Instructional aides are also experienced teachers, but they lack learning handicapped credentials. The co-directors have extensive qualifications as reading specialists, school administrators, and learning disabilities teachers. A physician specializing in LD, a psychologist and a speech/language therapist are consultants to the staff.

Parents expect and are expected to take an active participatory role in the education of their children. Daily on-going evaluation is given each child, and weekly reports go home to parents. Quarterly evaluations and conferences are almost unnecessary, as parents feel comfortable in communicating with the school at any time. Grades are given to junior and senior high school students, and the school is empowered to grant diplomas to graduates.

There is certainly a wide mix in this school: mildly, moderately and severely learning disabled children, the gifted and others who could probably attend a regular school. But the diversity can be exciting and stimulating, and the program at the Center works effectively.

DALLAS ACADEMY
950 Tiffany Way Dr.
Dallas, TX 75218

Private/Coed
Day/Residential
Enrollment 65
Ages 13-19

Dallas Academy has had its growing pains just as have the 65 junior and senior high school coed LD students whom it currently serves. However, the educational intent and program have been of consistently high quality since the school's founding in 1968 by a former mayor of Dallas and a group of concerned Texan parents who could find no suitable schooling for their children. Despite many changes throughout the years, its prevailing hard work ethic seems likely to remain.

Located in a northeastern residential area and housed in a former church building too small to accommodate easily the school's extensive program offerings, this less than ideal setting still manages to get the job done. A nearby "Y" is rented to provide swimming and physical education, and students are transported there for those classes. Ten students are boarders and live four miles away at a Baptist Children's Home under the supervision of seminarians. These students are permitted to have cars and part-time jobs, but regular van service to and from the school is available as needed. The day students commute on their own or pay for the school bus service.

The $4,400 tuition and $5,600 boarding fee, plus some endowment income, fairly well cover the costs. Eleven children have some form of scholarship. Neither the Board nor parents are expected to help with fund-raising. Parental cooperation in the form of assuming a supportive role and fostering realistic expectations is required for students to be admitted. Report cards with grades of A, B, C or incomplete are sent to parents every six weeks, conferences are held when needed, and in the spring results of formal standardized testing are shared. The school deemphasizes testing, focusing instead on what needs to be done to get the child through a course with a passing grade. This pragmatic approach is evident in the admissions procedure. Previous test data and academic records are evaluated to confirm the existence of a learning/reading disability and the non-existence of a severe emotional disturbance. During the required interview, attitude is assessed, and some informal testing may be done to determine placement. Otherwise, school time is spent on fulfilling the minimum graduation requirements for a state approved high school diploma.

The major thrust of Dallas Academy actually is to build a strong work ethic within each student so that those children who have learned to avoid working and meeting responsibilities will instead strive to put forth the extra effort so necessary to achieve their potential. While many students go on to college, that is not the school's primary goal. Realistic understanding by each student of how his handicap or disability affects his life is stressed. Students are not given a choice about meeting the requirements set for them, but as they begin to experience success, behavioral and attitudinal changes occur which make perseverance less onerous. In most basic subjects individual work contracts are set up, but science and social studies are taught on a group basis. A full range of academic courses is offered as well as electives in drama, typing, art, choir, health, drafting, sewing and driver education. Nearly 80 percent take some sort of elective reading program. For an additional fee individual tutoring and private music lessons are also available.

The present staff is made up of eight full-time teachers, two part-time reading specialists, two part-time language therapists (who are trained in the Orton-Gillingham method), a part-time music therapist, an art specialist, a part-time social worker and a nurse. About half have their Master's degree; four are fully certified in LD. The staff works together in the spirit of a team. Since certain changes were instituted three years ago, morale and staff retention have been high. The departure of the school's principal to pursue an advanced degree will, it is hoped, mean no change in the dynamics of the Dallas Academy's program. The replacement whom she hired is committed to ensuring a continuation.

Incomplete work means staying at school on Friday afternoons while the other children take off for home or special activities. When disruptive classroom behavior affects others negatively, a crisis intervention teacher removes the child from the classroom until he is back in control. Occasionally, there will be in-school suspension which the director supervises. Generally, positive reinforcement is the mode of behavior management. Responsible actions mean privileges; these may take the form of an off-campus lunch with a teacher or participation in camping, canoeing or skiing trips. There are practically no drop-outs any more; some may leave because of custody problems following divorce, but satisfaction with the school seems otherwise high. A parent of a commuter praised the Academy, saying that the staff appears to *love* the students, is extremely dedicated and works very hard to help them develop organizational skills and knowledge about their individual learning needs and styles. Whereas college had once seemed out of the question, her son was now planning to attend Southern Methodist University.

A fifth year post-high school program permits attendance at a local junior college. Those for whom college is inappropriate often may receive funds for later training through the Vocational Rehabilitation Commission. Nearly half of the students stay four to five years and graduate; the rest return to public schools before that time. No one seems to depart without first having overcome the problems that brought him to the Academy in the first place. As one residential student put it, he came knowing he had abilities but feeling he couldn't achieve. Two years later, he was no longer anxious, he'd pulled his grades up from D's and F's to A's and B's, he could concentrate, and he could get along with his peers. He credited the personal, caring attention he'd received with making the difference.

DENVER ACADEMY
235 S. Sherman
Denver, Colorado 80209

Private/Coed
Day/Residential
Enrollment 160
Ages 8-17

Master teaching is the hallmark of the Denver Academy. The other distinguishing feature of this private school in the Colorado state capital is its wholehearted commitment to the proposition that learning disabled adolescents with close to average intelligence or better and no primary social/emotional disturbance will experience significant positive growth if provided with an appropriate program.

This professional premise and prowess have, since the school's founding in 1972, enabled more than 1,000 adolescent boys and girls to "make it" academically.

Half of the 160 students at the Academy are boarders who come from elsewhere in the United States and abroad. These students are assigned to live with one of 20 families chosen for their previous success in parenting and in providing a suitably structured home environment. This residential arrangement has worked so effectively that it doubtless will be retained, even though the Denver Academy might acquire its own new facility and campus upon completion of a capital improvement program. Until then, the Academy will occupy a leased, former Catholic school in a pleasant Denver neighborhood. The tuition cost is $4,500. The boarding fee is an additional $4,500 for the 172 day school year.

Dr. Paul Knott, the school's director as well as a clinical psychologist and one of Denver Academy's three founders, heads a teaching staff of three associate directors — each of whom teaches a class — and 32 "master teachers." In addition, six interns, ten full- or part-time aides, student teachers from nearby universities and parent volunteers take part in the instructional program. All but the starting nucleus of the regular staff had preparatory work at the Academy during a teacher-internship program lasting a minimum of two years and consisting of on-the-job, post-graduate training in classroom management and structure, student counseling and discipline, multisensory techniques and individualization methods. Interns are gradually weaned from their mentors and given greater responsibility, but before being promoted to a staff position they must demonstrate competence in all areas of teaching.

Nearly all of the teaching faculty have a Master's degree, and 27 are certified in LD. Turnover is extremely low, in part because of the salary schedule, but also because of the reputation and status the faculty enjoys. The Denver Academy staff serve frequently as educational consultants and have set up training programs and two model schools outside of Colorado.

Though ungraded, the Academy provides a fully individualized, full curriculum at all grade levels. Approximately ten students of comparable chronological age are in each classroom along with the teacher and either an aide or an intern. The basics, in language development and in mathematics, are stressed and taught on a one-to-one basis or in small groups of three to five. The individually prescribed instruction is designed so that each child experiences a high degree of success and is challenged to move ahead. Walking this tightrope with every youngster every day is considered essential to "successful instruction and confidence building."

The best of contemporary research is utilized in program planning. For language instruction, students are assessed and classified during the first month of school and placed within five major diagnostic categories, using two variables as placement determinants: the student's ability to learn inductively and his level of success on visual aptitude tests. The five categories, although acknowledged by the staff as simplistic and not all-inclusive, are (1) dyslexic, (2) secondary language problem (SL), (3) educationally handicapped (EH), (4) dysphonetic and (5) attentional deficits. The dyslexics are taught directly the structure and science of language by means of a strong, systematic phonics program. The second category benefits from a systematic linguistic text and requires little drill except in spelling. The educationally handicapped profit from intrinsic phonics instruction, the reading of good literature, and the self-corrected pre-test and study techniques recommended by Bradley Loomer (1978). The dysphonetics need help with their auditory skills, and, depending on their inductive ability, a whole language method or a Fernald approach is used. Those with attentional deficits may fall into the gifted LD category, but they need help with word meaning and problem solving strategies.

The school's mathematics program is not predicated on the preceding diagnostic categories. Dyslexic students may experience no difficulty in math except with word problems. Since learning styles do vary, some students, upon the recommendation of the coordinator, may receive remedial help using Montessori techniques. Math groups change daily depending on the nature of problems encountered. Once basic math skills are mastered, students are placed in consumer math and/or algebra classes.

A range of "integrative courses" is offered in more than a dozen subject matter areas. These approximate the content of courses offered in conventional schools, but, in these, language skills are reinforced. Auditory, visual and kinesthetic processes are a part of all presentations. The emphasis is on teaching students how to transfer their skills and to make these functional so that they have the survival and compensatory skills crucial to returning successfully to a regular classroom setting.

There is no separate reading department at the Denver Academy. Reading is taught across the board by every teacher and is an integral part of the primary instruction provided in the language program. At Denver, reading success is as highly valued as athletic success. A student who reads five books receives gratis a blue Academy T-shirt. For reading ten he gets a green one, for 15 a brown one and for 20 a black shirt, thus paralleling the belt system of the martial arts. "The exciting part of this program is that it works." say Academy officials. "Students who refused to read are now reading for leisure."

Progress reports are issued quarterly with the usual A,B,C,D and F evaluations. In the various subject areas, specific skills are evaluated along with attitude, effort and social behavior. Standardized achievement tests are given twice yearly. In addition, at least six parent conferences are scheduled during the school year.

About 150 students are considered in order to fill the 60 or so vacancies for the upcoming year. The kind of entrance tests required is constantly evaluated and often changes. The student body is rather heterogeneous. Although most are between 13 and 17, there are some who are as young as eight. Typically, most students spend between two to four years at the Academy. Its goal for them is that they "obtain a high degree of self-discipline and responsibility before they leave." That might or might not mean they would later be college bound. There is a college preparatory track for those who have earned their way in through earlier academic masteries. The curriculum includes some ongoing remedial instruction but, generally, is designed along the lines of Mortimer Adler's *Paiedeia Proposal* (1982).

The combination of a competent teacher and a sound rationale goes far to reduce or eliminate discipline problems. Positiveness with firmness is the guiding principal in Academy classrooms. When students need to be reprimanded or punished, someone whom the student perceives as warm and caring — purportedly the teacher — takes care of the misbehavior. Before being hired, all teachers learn a proper intervention procedure which often consists of only a quickly issued warning or a modification of a student's work load. Repeated misconduct mandates that a student "take that behavior to the wall." Most go quietly when told. Counterbalancing this procedure is the positive stroking for appropriate behavior. Built-up pressure is released in *values classes* where complaints are aired three times a week or through participation in a wide variety of extracurricular sports activities.

Besides the Academy's critical program components of teacher-training, mastery of the "basics," researched strategies and integrative learning, there is the structure principle. Structure is everywhere evident: in the classroom where students are put to work immediately after entering and kept on task until dismissal; in discussion which prescribes that students not speak until acknowledged by the teacher; in any situation where staff and a student's peers are relating and doing so with mutual respect. New students are so busy at first that they have no unplanned time. Once these students have internalized the structure and the reasoning behind it and are ready for more advanced work, they progress to more permissive settings.

Recently a follow-up study was done which compared a random sample of former students who had attended for at least two years between the ages of 13 and 18 with a group of students who had similar traits except that they chose not to attend the Academy after being accepted.

The Academy students fared consistently better as college students, employees and fully self-supporting adults. Results such as these, plus the spontaneously expressed endorsements of parents and past students, give credence to the Academy's claim that master teaching is the heart and soul of their program by which means LD adolescents become "confident, productive, forward-looking individuals."

THE FROSTIG CENTER
OF EDUCATIONAL THERAPY
2495 E. Mountain St.
Pasadena, CA. 91104

Private/Coed
Day & Tutoring
Enrollment 74
Ages 3-18.

Frostig is a school that has been in trouble, but signs indicate that things might be getting better. Some thirty years ago, Dr. Marianne Frostig opened her heart and her home to help children with severe learning difficulties. She developed a concept that has since evolved into a "moving testimony to the power of an individual to make a difference in the world." This pioneer in the field of learning disabilities founded a school which is still placed among noteworthy schools for the learning disabled. According to a 1978 follow-up study, three fourths of the students polled graduated from high school and forty percent pursued their education beyond high school, an impressive record for former failures! But Dr. Frostig now spends much of her time on the lecture circuit, and the Center has withstood frequent administrative turnover as well as a significant shift in the nature of its LD population, as the scramble for funded students necessitated the acceptance of severely behaviorally disturbed LD children. Fifty-eight percent of Frostig students were funded in the 1982-1983 school year. The school has operated at two sites. However, these are to be consolidated, a new director appointed, and the more troublesome, "acting out" student excluded.

The student body consisted of 74 full-time day students from primary grades through high school, plus 30 children in a tutoring program, during the spring of 1983. The new Pasadena campus, acquired in 1980, will accommodate the 1983 consolidation. It is situated in a quiet residential neighborhood right across the street from the Tournament of Roses Park. This former parochial school contains well-maintained classrooms, administration offices, a diagnostic clinic, a large, fully equipped kitchen, a dining room, a gymnasium and a church which will one day become an auditorium.

The 42 students who attend the Pasadena campus are placed in one of six classrooms: one preschool, one primary, two elementary, one junior and one senior high school group. The average class size ranges from five to eight students; a teacher and an assistant are in each room. All children are given a basic academic foundation as well as perceptual, movement and language training and adaptive physical education. Thus, Frostig not only teaches academic subjects but also develops the underlying skills which, if not acquired, undermine the child's ability to learn.

The day school program is truly a multidisciplinary approach which treats the whole child. Highly trained educational therapists, i.e., teachers, work closely with specialists at the Center in speech and language, movement, psychology, visual perception and social work.

157

Thus, a Frostig social studies unit is not just a social studies unit. It incorporates math and reading, social and emotional factors, perceptual activities, gross and fine motor skills. The educational therapist knits all of these components together to provide the youngster with a complete learning experience, not just a cognitive one. This methodology is utilized throughout the day over and over again.

For a school as financially well endowed as Frostig, very few electives or extracurricular activities are offered, not even computer training. A teen rap-group does meet once a week, its primary function being to develop skills in social interaction and decision making. An elementary program in "guided imagery and relaxation" helps the child to release his creativity, to develop relaxation techniques, to discard his feelings of past failures and to become more open.

Children stay a minimum of two years. Some, especially those with severe emotional or family problems, may spend their entire school career at Frostig. A comprehensive evaluation is required for each child before admission. This evaluation must show the child to be LD, mild to severe. If the child does not have a previous evaluation by the district school or an outside agency, the Center's diagnostic clinic will perform the testing for a $500 fee. The clinic also provides one-to-one speech and language therapy, motor movement and perceptual training for a fee of $25 per hour. Individual counseling is available for $48 per hour. For family and group therapy, fees are individually determined.

Frostig is more than a special school; it is a training center and a laboratory that investigates the intricate process of learning. The Center is active in training teachers in special education techniques and serves as a research facility to study the causes and treatment of learning problems. The institution is fortunate to be able to afford these extras; its sizeable endowment is $1,900,000. Much of this money is tagged for research, but the Center does offer $80,000 in scholarships annually to offset the rather high, by California standards, $8,000 tuition.

Likewise, teachers are more than teachers at Frostig; they are trained "educational therapists." All have California learning handicapped credentials and are required to attend frequent, special in-service workshops offered during the school year and to train with Dr. Frostig and her associate, Dr. Phyllis Maslow, during the summer. A teacher may become a master teacher after being trained at the Center in the Frostig approach. Besides the 12 regular classroom teachers, there are a speech and language therapist, an adaptive physical education teacher, a movement specialist and a crisis intervention counselor to serve the school. As the school is a training center, several local colleges and universities sponsor internship programs there. A separate staff of four tutors serves 30 students who are enrolled in schools elsewhere but who come for extra help in order to "catch up." The fee for this program is $25 per hour. A separate psychoeducational clinic, staffed by three clinical psychologists, a clinical social worker, two educational diagnosticians and a school psychologist, provides diagnostic evaluation and therapy for children and families of the school or community.

Parents need no formal invitation to visit the school and talk with teachers. A comprehensive parent education program schedules speakers on the average of once a month, arranges parent counseling and informs parents of children's progress. Formal parent/teacher conferences are held twice a year and extensive progress reports are sent to parents three times a year. In addition, students take standardized achievement tests every spring. The results are sent home.

Frostig is a venerable institution and has gone a long way on its reputation. It is presently difficult to determine the true state of affairs in the classroom. Only the future will tell whether Frostig's quality will equal that of earlier days.

ITOP CENTER FOR LEARNING
23133 Orange Ave.
El Toro, CA 92630

Private/Coed
Day & Tutoring
Enrollment 50
Ages 5-15

ITOP (Individual Task Oriented Program) started as a tutoring service in a three-bedroom home in 1957. Sister Paula Jane, the program's founder, believed a gap existed between what was available and what certain disadvantaged children deserved. Since that time, the school has grown and now accommodates 50 boys and girls from elementary through high school grades in an all-day program. Other children and adults attend the separate tutoring facility.

ITOP serves children who collectively manifest the full range of learning disabilities as well as 12 non-handicapped children who need a structured, controlled environment in order to achieve. These latter children might actually have some diagnosable form of learning handicap, but it is felt that those with a specific LD benefit from association with underachievers in need of ITOP's services and that they do very well together.

The school's quarters are certainly not elegant. Portable, temporary trailer coaches are being used as classrooms until money can be raised to build a permanent facility on the one-acre site just purchased outside of San Juan Capistrano. Even though the coaches are crowded, there is no cramped feeling, a feat of nun-like organization and efficiency. The four classrooms, while small, prove adequate for the 12 to 14 children, the teacher and her aide. A large multipurpose room, the only extra space available outside the classrooms, is used for less structured activities and computer training.

The children work diligently on their *Individually Designed Task Oriented Programs* (daily classwork). Each teacher gives her students some type of reward for academic excellence and responsible behavior, and all children earn either a gold star, a balloon or a point each day. Here and there, the awards all add up on the artistic, creative display boards pinned to the walls of the classrooms. Classes are ungraded and divided into a lower primary, higher primary and two intermediate groups. The reading program used at ITOP is PIRK — Perceptual Integration Reading Kit, a basic multisensory linguistic patterning approach much like the Slingerland method. Only fun, creative, homework is assigned, for the faculty believes that otherwise these assignments become punishment for the parent and accomplish little.

There are not many amenities in this school; the emphasis is on the basics. Art and music are each offered once a week and physical education is taught three times. There is neither a science lab nor a gymnasium, and the library is in the multi-purpose room. Children and parents arrange their own transportation. No "free lunch" is provided; the old-fashioned brown paper bag is definitely in style. Despite its space limitations, ITOP is a happy place.

Sister Paula Jane and her staff delight in telling of the successes they have had with their children. The case of thirteen-year-old Jeffrey is but one example of the many tales told. Jeffrey came to ITOP in the spring of 1982 from a public school. He had autistic tendencies and was academically dysfunctional. The following spring, Jeffrey was reading 7th grade material and solving 5th grade fraction problems. As his self-confidence grew, he began to relate to and converse with students and staff.

An all female staff operates the program. Sister Paula Jane has a Master's degree in linguistics and has taught in that field from elementary grades through the college level. All teachers and the building principal have California learning handicapped credentials; the principal holds a Master's degree in special education.

Formal parent/teacher conferences and extensive written evaluations are given three times per year. Parents, however, are encouraged to call or visit the school at any time for a more informal discussion with their child's teacher. All parents pay $5,000 per student per year.

In spite of a continuing search and struggle for space "which is more precious than gold," the school is on the right road and looks to the future with optimism. Often it is said, "Let us pray." Indeed, some patron saint of little children might inspire a wealthy benefactor so that this deserving program can settle down in its own building on its own land.

LANDMARK WEST SCHOOL
11450 Port Rd.
Culver City, CA 90230

Private/Coed
Day
Enrollment 40
Ages 8-17

This new day school which opened in September, 1983, with 30 elementary and 10 high school boys and girls will mirror on a smaller scale the fine program of its counterpart, Lardmark East.

Landmark West is a program of the Learning Disabilities Foundation of Prides Crossing, Massachusetts. This private, non-profit organization is concerned with all aspects of learning disabilities and has conducted programs for dyslexic young people since 1956.

The Foundation initiated Landmark West at the request of California parents whose children had attended classes at Landmark in Massachusetts.

The school, located in a residential area of Culver City, outside Los Angeles, occupies 27,000 square feet of rented space in a former public school. The building is large; it will take a few years to fill it up. In addition to the many classrooms, there are a gymnasium, art rooms, a huge auditorium and outside athletic fields.

David Drake, son of the founder of the original Landmark, is determined to carry on the same outstanding program with the same type of student that made the Eastern school the largest learning disabilities institution in the nation. Although quite similar to the Massachusetts prototype, the range of programs will be limited, because West is a day program and smaller in size.

The core of the program is the daily one-to-one tutorial which focuses on reading, spelling, composition and handwriting. In addition, a class in language arts concentrates on writing skills; an auditory oral expression class addresses the characteristic difficulties of dyslexic students in following oral directions, notetaking from dictation, auditory discrimination of certain sounds and oral composition. Classes in mathematics, physical education, social studies, science and art are also required. Classes are small, averaging six with a maximum of eight pupils.

The ungraded Landmark West School emphasizes achievement rather than grade placement. Each student's program is individually designed with skill-building content material appropriate to the student's age.

Landmark West has a strong academic supervisory system. Each tutorial and all classes are guided by the director of education and three academic supervisors whose job it is to observe students in class and advise teachers on strategies and resources. Thirteen teachers now make up the staff. The entire group meets daily during the school week to share insights, discuss individual students and coordinate approaches.

Criteria for admission to West are the same as those for East. Only those youngsters of average intelligence, with demonstratable ability to learn and an identifiable learning disability, but no primary emotional problems, are eligible to enroll. According to the headmaster, these criteria will be strictly observed. He expects few, if any, funded students at West. Drake insists that his school cannot accommodate the behaviorally disturbed youngster that most California schools are required to take to acquire district funding. So, any parents sending their child to Landmark West can expect to pay the $8,300 tuition.

PARK CENTURY SCHOOL
2040 Stoner Ave.
Los Angeles, CA 90025

Private/Coed
Day
Enrollment 40
Ages 5-13

An excellent small school in West Los Angeles, Park Century has been in operation for 15 years and offers an effective elementary school LD program in spacious new facilities accommodating 40 boys and girls. Although tuition is high - $12,500 - the school is somewhat unique among California schools visited in that it offers a daily one-to-one tutorial.

Park Century is located in a far from pastoral setting; it is in an industrial area. Concrete extends in all directions, affording no real outdoor playground. Inside the excellently designed single story building, however, there is plenty of space. The five classrooms are large enough to accommodate eight children and still allow room for structured play activity and moveable seating arrangements, plus plenty of books, materials and educational toys. Separate tutoring rooms, a small children's library, a larger multipurpose room, a kitchen, conference rooms and administration offices occupy the rest of the building.

School is in session from 9 AM until 2 PM each day. Busing is provided for funded students; others arrive by public transportation or parent-initiated car pools. Children bring their lunches or eat at a nearby restaurant where, according to one child, "the food is great."

Classes are structured according to age, academic achievement and social maturity with one teacher and one aide. Movement between groups takes place whenever the child shows sufficient academic skill to allow him entrance to a higher skill level. Each child has a set of individual goals determined by his math and reading tutors and his classroom teacher. Goals are written not only for the academic subjects but for social/emotional development and work habits as well. Each child meets for 20 minutes daily with his reading specialist on a one-to-one basis. Individual tutoring in arithmetic is provided for a total of 60 minutes per week in either three 20-minute periods, two 30-minute periods or one 60-minute session with follow-up in the classroom. The classroom teacher instructs classes in language, social studies, study skills and science and acts as an adjunct for the reading and mathematics tutorials. Cooking classes and art classes are given in a multipurpose kitchen which also functions as a science laboratory. Computers and computer literacy classes are on the school's "wish list." Physical education classes are held every day in a nearby park or in the school's multipurpose room.

The staff includes five classroom teachers, five aides, tutors, a speech and language therapist who visits selected children twice a week and a physical education teacher who spends part of her time working on a one-to-one basis with children needing perceptual motor skills development. A teacher comes twice a week for a music program which is incorporated into the all-school play given each year in June. Ginny Shain and Gail Tabb have been with the school since its inception in 1968, working as classroom teachers and assistant co-directors until appointed as co-directors by the school's Board of Governors in 1976. Most of the teaching and tutoring staff have Master's degrees in special education. They do not use any one specific approach in their teaching, for they are experienced enough to be able to pick and choose the most appropriate method. Similarily, the reading tutor will employ whatever works best for the child — either a linguistics, sight word or phonics method. The school makes use of materials specifically designed for LD students, but it also incorporates into the classroom the standard materials used in the public schools so that the child will have an easier time when being reintegrated into the non-remedial schools. Further, the staff at Park Century works closely with the child's psychiatrist, psychologist or social worker whose visits to the school are considered vital to developing the communication necessary "in planning a child's program, responding to his behavior, and dealing with his feelings and the feelings of his family."

Thirty percent of the students are funded by their districts, and some of these children are labeled SED (severely emotionally disturbed). But, Park Century believes that with the development of a positive self-image, social skills and satisfying peer relationships, the behavior problems will be ameliorated in time. When behavior problems do occur, they are handled individually. There is no set discipline procedure. If intervention by the teacher is not sufficient, a full-time person is available to work with severe discipline problems. A time-out room also serves those children who need to calm down a bit and to get away from the stresses of the classroom and the other children. This room is not used as a punishment; it is meant to play a therapeutic role in behavior management.

Park Century believes that "family involvement is an essential ingredient in the success of a youngster with learning problems." Parent activities, such as mothers' groups and evening seminars, are held regularly to provide educational information and emotional support. Three parent conferences are held each year, standardized academic testing is done twice a year and a lengthy pupil-progress report is sent to parents in March.

Weekly, on-going staffings determine a child's movement from one group to another within the school and his readiness to return to a regular school setting. His academic level, work habits and social skills are the criteria for out-placements; the staff helps to find the appropriate new non-remedial facility. Classroom teachers visit prospective schools and then coordinate with the selected school to ensure a smooth transition. Supportive tutoring is available, if necesssary, in the school's after-school tutoring program. Regular contact with graduates is maintained, and many times these graduates return to Park Century and share their success stories with the youngsters.

A verse on the Park Century's colorful brochure aptly illustrates the plight of the learning disabled child whom this school claims to be 95 percent successful in helping:

Star light
Star bright
First star I see tonight
I wish I may
I wish I might
Learn to add and read and write

RASKOB LEARNING INSTITUTE
3520 Mountain Blvd.
Oakland, CA 94619

Private/Coed
Day & Tutoring
Enrollment 24
Ages 8-13

A first-rate school is located high up in the hills overlooking Oakland on the lovely, secluded campus of Holy Name College. The facilities are spacious, which is unusual for most California special schools, and there is an aura of tranquility about the place. The Raskob Foundation provided seed money to a Catholic nun in 1960 to start this program, but Raskob functions as a private, non-sectarian institution today.

Raskob offers two programs — a part-time tutoring service and a full-time day school. The Learning Institute offers throughout the day and evening individual and small group lessons lasting 60 to 90 minutes to children or adults. For the 15-week spring and fall periods, instruction is given twice a week. In the six-week summer program, lessons are four times weekly. Fees range from $11 to $22 per hour and are determined on the basis of the number of students in the group. Between 100 and 120 students attend the Institute each semester. A second program, which operates independently from the Institute, is the full-time day school serving boys and girls between the ages of 8 and 13. Admission is based on a diagnostic evaluation, both academic and psychological, which is administered either by an outside agency or at the school's clinic.

Students in both the day school and the Institute are commuters from the Oakland-Berkley areas. As public transportation is not readily available and Raskob provides no bus service, children must arrange on their own to get to and from school each day. The $4,725 tuition is not exorbitant, and the school is filled to capacity. A limited number of partial scholarships are available from an endowment fund and through fund raising by parents. Raskob once had over one-half of its population funded by school districts, but because fewer and fewer LD students are being funded, now only three receive tuition reimbursement. This seems not to have hurt Raskob, since total enrollment has increased. The reason, according to the director, is that parents want a more individual program and a more personal approach for their children who are having trouble coping in the public school. Moreover, they are willing to pay for it. As one parent stated: "Before my child came here, he was lost in that school (public)...even in the resource room the teacher didn't have enough time to give to the 30 children she was responsible for ... he didn't have a real individual program, all the kids were doing the same work."

Parents are highly involved in a variety of activities. They might be found fund raising, transporting children to the field trips taken around the area or attending many of the evening social and educational meetings. Conferences are scheduled three times per year, but most of the parents are in weekly communication with the staff.

The school does a remarkable job with the income from its relatively low tuition. As long as it can continue to give quality education at the present price, it will. To raise tuition would only "layer out certain families whose children should be here," states the director.

The all female staff is highly qualified and experienced. The majority of teachers at the day school and Institute hold a Master's degree in special education and have been with Raskob from four to 18 years. The two teaching assistants are experienced college graduates.

Two classrooms, each containing 12 children, one master teacher and a teaching assistant, serve the 24 children enrolled in the day program. The rooms are large, bright and airy with many books and materials in evidence. While programs are structured individually for each student in reading, mathematics and language arts, children work in groups in the content areas of geography, history and science. These classes are deliberately structured to provide a student the opportunity to interact with his peers and to wean him from the idea that he will always have a teacher by his side.

Art is incorporated into the school program during the day, and there is also an after-school art program. A full-time music teacher instructs the children in the Orff-Schulwerk method of music movement. The school uses the Holy Name College gymnasium, pool and soccer field in its physical education program. Because physical fitness is stressed, not competitive games, the school does not field teams. Emphasis is placed on the President's Fitness Program with pre- and post-tests being given each year to determine gains made in fitness and gross motor development.

Raskob is operating in the black and doing well. It does not have to scramble for funds from local school districts, and a full enrollment allows the school to choose only those students it feels will benefit.

SABIN-McEWEN LEARNING INSTITUTE
P.O. Box 22292
Carmel, CA 93922

Private/Coed
Day & Tutoring
Enrollment 18
Ages 8-13

It's back to the one-room schoolhouse in the tourist town of Carmel-by-the-Sea. The Sabin-McEwen Institute, which basically operates out of a single room, has a dual program. It is both a half-day school that operates on a shared-time basis with the child's regular school and an after-school tutoring program for children and adults. The day school tuition is $5,000; a $24 per hour fee is charged for tutoring. The State Certified class for eight boys and girls between the ages of 8 and 13 meets daily from 8 AM to noon. During this time, the children, who exhibit a full range of learning disabilities and expressive language difficulties, receive a straight academic program devoted to the acquisition of basic skills. The "frills" are left to the regular afternoon schools. This is a splendid idea which gives children the best of both worlds. They receive necessary individual instruction at the Institute and enjoy the enrichment and normal school setting of the larger private or public school.

This class is located in a room of a former school just a shade tree away from downtown Carmel. The large room is divided into several areas where a master teacher and her two assistants work, each with a few children. The school is too small to have any extra support staff, but an occupational therapist and psychologist are available for consultation.

The $5,000 tuition is low for a school that provides three teachers for eight students. Sabin-McEwen's teacher-pupil ratio compares favorably with expensive Eastern schools that believe that the smaller the group, the better the learning.

Extensive academic testing by the Institute is required before admission. The planning of the child's individual program is based on this full battery of tests. While no one method is used in teaching reading, a decoding, phonetic approach similar to the Orton-Gillingham method is usually followed.

Many new schools are short lived; this is a new school, having only opened its doors in 1982. But as it is the only program on the Monterey Peninsula and provides a much needed service in a rather unique fashion, there is every reason to believe it will endure.

STARPOINT SCHOOL
Texas Christian University
Fort Worth, TX 76129

Private/Coed
Day
Enrollment 40
Ages 6-10

College students and instructors regularly trek across the Texas Christian University campus in Fort Worth, Texas, to observe and participate in classes at a strikingly attractive elementary school. There, at Starpoint School, 40 children between the ages of six and ten pursue their lessons unperturbed by the studious scrutiny of these visitors and fellow students. Starpoint is outstandingly suited to accommodate both groups, for it was designed and built expressly for the instruction of learning disabled youngsters of primary age and the training of special education teachers.

A former University Board President and his wife, whose grandson was learning disabled, supplied the impetus for the school's founding. For ten years the school was housed in a barracks while the staff experimented with various curricular and architectural alternatives. The present Starpoint facility is a four-year-old showplace which incorporates the best of those ideas, plus the decorator touches of interior design classes at TCU.

Four color-coordinated classrooms, each serving a different age group, flank a central assembly room with a carpeted pit. Offices, a conference room, teachers' lounge and resource area are at the front of the building. At the back are a classroom for the TCU students, a workroom-library, a multipurpose gymnasium, a kitchen and lunchroom. All equipment, materials and accessories are attractively and carefully placed according to plan. However, within each classroom the formica-topped, trapezoidal-shaped desks are being constantly rearranged.

The goal of this private day school is to provide ways for children to experience success in learning and to grow in self-esteem. Students are thoroughly screened prior to admission to be sure that they are in the average to above average intelligence range and have no serious emotional or behavioral problems. Students come from all over the greater Fort Worth area, but none are tuition-reimbursed. The cost of a year's tuition at Starpoint is $1,800. This represents only part of the actual cost of the program, since the budget and the major portion of the funds are provided and controlled by TCU. Thanks to some direct fund raising by the principal and a TCU scholarship program, some families pay as little as $50 per month. Almost twice as many students as there are vacancies are considered for admission. They may be dismissed if their attendance is not regular or if they manifest severe and unmanageable behavior problems.

Teacher-directed group work is the primary learning mode. Within each age and ability grouping, the instructional objectives are broken down into small incremental steps. Instruction is multisensory and didactic involving group discovery, oral responses, written follow-up and considerable review. Gradually children are given larger amounts of individualized work until by the end of their last year at Starpoint they are working on a totally personalized program while still within the group. Positive reinforcement at all stages is the means for encouraging progress and handling discipline. Homework is given regularly, but it is not expected to take more than 15 minutes and is used for teaching responsibility and reviewing work. Tutoring is available for absentees who have fallen behind. Outings to places such as the theater or nature center are scheduled about once a month. The school does not often make instructional use of the library or the two available computer terminals. Much of the curriculum was developed at the school. For reading, for example, the public school materials (Macmillan) are used but are supplemented by a phonics-oriented language program that stresses a lot of review and overlearning.

Working with the parents of the Starpoint students is considered crucial to the success of the program. During the four annual parent conferences, the child's work, needs, progress and standarized test scores are discussed in detail. Parents are expected to understand the world of testing. In 1983-1984, parents must take a course taught by a TCU behavioral psychologist. Input from the active parent organization is welcome and particularly helpful in working out school transportation difficulties.

The school staff consists of three teachers and one teaching director, who is also the principal. These four all have their Master's in special education and are fully certified in LD. Each year, a Starpoint Associate (who is a TCU Master's degree candidate) begins a two-year staff appointment. The support services staff includes a clinical psychologist, a consulting pediatrician and a behavioral psychologist. The use of medication to control behavioral problems or to enable children to learn is viewed favorably, and the school can avail itself of the nearby TCU medical facilities. Members of the TCU staff arrange the programming of physical education, art, music and speech communication classes. Besides, TCU student teachers perform a variety of tasks at the school. The regular teachers are educational diagnosticians, and they work together as a team in an enthusiastic and professional manner. They routinely draw upon the resources of the support staff to help diagnose needs and prescribe work.

The recommended placement for children who leave Starpoint is third grade. It is felt that children often need a year to adjust to a new school setting and repeating a grade is a good way to meet this need. Some children return to either regular or special education classes in public schools; others continue in private schools. Three former Starpoint students are now enrolled at TCU, and several are operating their own businesses.

Apparently this lab school is pointed in the right direction. The special education department at TCU and the teachers it trains reap many benefits from their association with Starpoint. So also do the children who attend, their parents, and all others who believe that effective early intervention is necessary to prevent the disabling effects of LD later in life.

STERNE SCHOOL
2690 Jackson
San Francisco, CA 94115

Private/Coed
Day & Tutoring
Enrollment 58
Ages 9-18

No fancy brochures advertise this gracious, little school located in a nice, residential area of San Francisco. Prospective enrollees receive a plain pamphlet containing an application for admission and a set of school rules. Yet Sterne is potentially a superior school that bears watching. With its well-dressed students attending quiet structured classes in an elegant three-story mansion, this school conveys the flavor of its Eastern counterparts.

Sterne opened in 1976 to teach ten LD children. Since then, its enrollment has increased to 58, with 39 students in the elementary grades and 19 in the high school. Because admission is based upon an evaluation by an outside agency, Sterne does not have its own diagnostic clinic. The school accepts children with normal or above intelligence. However, a youngster with widely discrepant scores on the WISC-R is eligible for admission if the staff feels he can process the amount of oral information to be given. Sterne's population comes from the San Francisco area, and 50 percent are funded by the student's home district. The school has minimal support staff so it cannot accept children with unmanageable behavior problems or children with severe communicative disorders or severe learning problems. All students must be able to fit into one of the existing groups which are based on age, social maturity and academic level.

Even with its low tuition of $3,600 to $4,300, Sterne has a scholarship program to help the 28 children not funded by their school districts. In 1982, three Sterne and five outside foundation scholarships were awarded.

The school's goal is to remediate but also to educate. For this reason there is a heavy emphasis on factual content in the history, geography and science classes. Another major tenet of the school's philosophy is that children must be able to function within a group. Students are age grouped in classes with individual attention being given to each within a group setting. Assignments for the group are tailored to individual skill levels. All academic classes for the elementary school are held in the morning from 9 AM to 12:30 PM with one mid-morning "nutrition break." Luncheon is taken in a nearby park. Afterwards, children take electives and physical education. Reading, writing and math classes for high school students are followed by afternoon work in science, geography, history and physical education. All students have one 50-minute, multisensory phonics-based reading period and a 45-minute mathematics class each day. Elective and content classes are scheduled for 40 minutes each. Six to eight children are in each elementary class, but the class size jumps to 12 in the junior and senior high school. One teacher, without the help of an aide, instructs each group. Writing is expected in every class, but one full 40-minute period is devoted to formal writing, sentence structure, paragraph development and composition. The school has two computers, and computer literacy is taught as an elective. Based upon staff expertise, a wide range of other elective courses, such as music, art, needlepoint, cooking, typing and archeology, are offered. Physical education classes are held in the nearby park with a much loved physical education teacher. This young college senior has a special affinity for the children he serves; he, too, is an LD student.

Helping the LD students and parents to understand and deal with learning disabilities is a major goal at Sterne. Once there is acceptance and understanding, the staff finds that a great deal of learning begins to take place as the children learn coping strategies necessary to enable them to participate fully in their world. The Sterne staff opens the right doors to invite these changes. All teachers are experienced in working with LD students, all are credentialed and most either have or are working toward their Master's degrees. Four of the seven teachers have been with the school since it opened. Even the director teaches every day. Because learning disabilities materials are available in the curriculum library, the staff may pick and choose those with which they feel most comfortable.

A weekly behavior evaluation program is a way, without reprimanding, of quietly encouraging the children to develop good behavior habits. Points are given daily in reading, math and homeroom classes for such good conduct as coming on time, being quiet or respectful, staying on task, following directions and minding one's own business. These points are totaled at the end of the week, and an appropriate reward is given. This efficient system enables children to monitor their own behavior.

Because students want grades, every nine weeks graded report cards are handed out, just as in regular schools. Teachers or parents may request conferences, and twice a year a progress report is sent to parents.

Sterne helps its students choose their next school and also provides an after-school program for its departees, who may return any day and participate in the after-school tutoring program. This plan assures a smoother than normal transition so that the receiving school does not bear the sole responsibility for educating the LD child. Sterne is also proud of the fact that of its 39 former students all but one are back in a traditional school setting and functioning very well.

Long ago, somebody said: "If you build a better mousetrap, the world will beat a path to your door." The Sterne School's dedicated, creative staff is building, year by year, a better school. Fortunate is the LD student who might someday find himself at Sterne's door.

WEST VALLEY—HILLSIDE EDUCATIONAL DEVELOPMENT CENTER
7041 Owensmouth Ave.
Canoga Park, CA 91303

Private/Coed
Day & Tutoring
Enrollment 38
Ages 7-15

Hillside Center is more than a day school; it also incorporates two centers for educational therapy, a diagnostic clinic and an after-school tutoring program. West Valley, the day school, serves 40 children ranging in age from 5 to 15 and offers an assortment of different remedial programs designed to fulfill the needs of three distinct groups. All five classes contain up to eight students, a teacher and an aide. Two of these classes contain only district funded students; one transitional class serves only non-funded students; and the other two are mixed, containing children in both categories.

Why this segregation? California school districts have lately been referring and funding children with severe emotional and behavioral problems to private schools. Here the more moderately learning handicapped need to be sequestered from the extremely disordered ones. To meet this need a transition class was initiated in 1982 at West Valley to oblige that "grey area" of LD students who qualify for neither funding nor special education classes in the public sector but who were under-achieving by one to two years in the crowded regular school classrooms. Eight are enrolled; the maximum of 15 may soon be reached.

The tuition for this latter program is $3,200, quite less than the $8,200 fee for the other four classes. Dr. Claude Hill, the school's mild-mannered and witty director, feels parents are willing to pay for LD education but are resentful when their youngsters are placed alongside the more disruptive funded students. West Valley wants to provide affordable, specialized schooling for these children.

In 1983-84 a dual program will be initiated enabling students to attend West Valley for remedial instruction and their local high school for enrichment, electives and social recreation.

Children accepted into the West Valley program must have the potential to function in the average or above average range of ability. The school will not accept the psychotic or autistic child. Before being accepted, a child is required to have a complete psychoeducational evaluation either by the Center's diagnostic clinic for a fee of $325 or by an outside agency.

West Valley is an odd-looking school. It operates in a business area of Canoga Park, out of two one-story modern buildings which look more like office suites than a school. Transportation is provided by a West Valley school bus. A school library is not considered a necessity, for use is made of the nearby public one. There is, however, a crisis room, painted pink because, according to Dr. Hill, pink produces placidity. Arts and crafts are taught in the regular classroom. Daily adaptive physical education classes are held at the school or in the local park. This little school actually defeated many larger schools to bring home the 1982 interscholastic football championship trophy. No fine arts, vocational or elective programs are offered. West Valley's expertise, in Hill's opinion, lies in teaching core "tool subjects."

In addition to the West Valley day school, two other sites, one in West Los Angeles and one in Sherman Oaks, California, provide individual 40 or 60 minute tutorials for children and adults in academics, sensory integration, speech, language and voice therapy. These Centers also provide parenting skills workshops and individualized counseling for students and families. Hourly tutoring fees range from $17.50 to $25; counseling fees are $40 per hour for those enrolled in the day school. Additional program fees vary according to the type and frequency of the program.

Dr. Hill has his background in educational psychology and formerly worked at the Marianne Frostig Center. A clinical director, who also comes from the Frostig Center, supervises all of the diagnostic work, and the after-school therapy programs. The teaching staff at West Valley includes five certified teachers and five aides, two full-time educational therapists who see individual students two or three times a week for 40- to 60-minute lessons, a part-time speech therapist, two psychologists and three part-time counselors.

The academic program at West Valley is not particularly structured. Classes are ungraded, and daily planning and teaching methods are left to the discretion of teachers. Programs are individualized to an extent, but group instruction prevails. Each day must include some reading, writing and spelling. Four parental conferences are arranged each year. These and the results from the two annual achievement tests keep parents informed as to the progress of their child. Because West Valley offers no accredited high school diploma, children must return to a regular school to graduate.

Fifty percent of the school population is funded at present, down from 75 percent in 1982, and the director feels there will be a further reduction by late 1984. He is confident that local school districts will develop programs exclusively for presently funded children. Even without any reductions, the West Valley school has pulled off a great balancing act in accommodating the funded and non-funded so well under the same roof.